GROWING SEASON:
Maturing of a Christian

Though this book is designed for group study, it is also intended for your personal enjoyment and spiritual growth. A leader's guide is available from your local bookstore or from your publisher.

Copyright 1990

Beacon Hill Press of Kansas City
Kansas City, Missouri

Printed in the United States of America
ISBN: 083-411-2760

Editor
Stephen M. Miller

Editorial Assistants
Becki Loar
Kathryn Roblee

Editorial Committee
Norman Campbell
Tom Mayse
Stephen M. Miller
Carl Pierce
Gene Van Note
Lyle Williams

15 14 13 12 11 10 9

Contents

Chapter 1

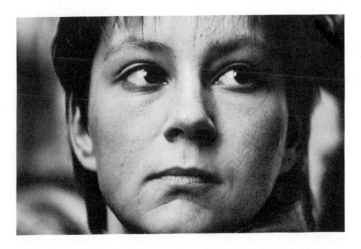

Take It from the Beginning

by Joseph Seaborn II

Background Scripture: Matthew 7:15-20; John 3:3-17;
Philippians 1:6

I SAT in a worship service that lasted over two hours. It took this long because of just one request the worship leader made: "Tell us how you came to know Christ."

• Bruce had been scared into his experience. The bushy-browed giant behind the podium had looked and sounded like a human thunderstorm. He preached a sermon that terrorized the congregation, for he preached about an angry God—a God so angry with sin He would condemn to hell anyone who had anything to do with it. Bruce said he felt he had only two options: Either go forward and meet the monster at the altar or go back and meet the devil at the door.

• Cindy had been sitting with her friend at a table in a sprawling university cafeteria. With silverware clinking around her and hundreds of voices chattering, she had bowed her head and asked Christ to give her "the change of a lifetime."

• Jim was alone in his pickup. The truck radio had conked out months before, but a portable FM receiver taped to the dash worked as well. He had been scanning the dial when he heard a voice that sounded familiar. He stopped to see if he could figure out whose it was. By the time Cliff Barrows came on to offer prayer at the end of the Billy Graham broadcast, Jim had already done what the speaker had suggested.

• For Barbara, the exact time was hard to nail down. She believed she had come to Christ in her early teens. But her tender age combined with three church services a week for as far back as she could remember had blurred her memory of the moment she had taken the step of faith.

At the end of this session, one thought stood out in my mind. In every case the life change began somewhere. But in no case did it happen the same way. A rampage by a frothing preacher, a conversation over lunch, a sermon by Billy Graham, an unremembered moment as a teen. God is certainly creative in the ways He uses to bring people to himself.

For every process of growth, there must be a beginning point. As one man in my church has said, "Anything that goes anywhere has to get started somewhere."

He's right. In the life of the soul, conversion to Christ is the starting point. Without it, all our attempts to mature into good people end up on the junk heap with our New Year's resolutions. But with conversion, a person is able to begin the venture of faith, confident that "he who began a good work in you will carry it on to completion" (Philippians 1:6).

Most people believe in God and are courteous toward Him. But belief and good manners aren't enough. At some point we must decide whether or not to commit the rest of our lives to Christ.

In spite of the fact that every person's conversion is unique, when you examine a number of these stories, you discover several parallels.

Born Bad

No matter if the people are from high society with a six-figure income, from middle-class suburbia with a paycheck-to-paycheck income, or from the ghetto with a poverty-level income, these people who turn to Christ have made the discovery they were born bad.

As hard as it is for our modern minds to accept, we are born spiritually warped. There is within the human spirit what some theologians call a bent to sinning. This bent comes with birth and shows up in time.

The very best human being you know may be a non-Christian who has volunteered in a nursing home, given to United Way, sponsored an overseas orphan, and cut his neighbor's grass. But that person still has a hidden tendency to veer away from God and toward his own selfish ways.

In conversion God empowers a person to resist this downward tug at the heart and, instead, turn toward God. Our inner tug-of-war, which has been favoring Satan, abruptly shifts in favor of God.

Writer James Denny phrased it well: "The very essence of Christianity is that it has the power to make bad men good." A sermon title by the Baptist preacher Harry Emerson Fosdick put it even more bluntly: "No Man Need Stay the Way He Is."

Ben Franklin may have been correct when he said, "God

helps those who help themselves," but in conversion God helps those who could never help themselves. By a single gift of forgiving grace, He clears up our sins from the past and gets us headed in a brand-new direction.

Conversion is the great traffic light of life. First, as a red light it requires us to stop our sinful ways of the past. And then it becomes a green light urging us on to a new life in Christ.

Loud Conversion, Quiet Conversion

If you sort through conversion stories to see what else they have in common, you will come upon a moment of crisis when the person made the leap of faith toward God. Not everyone will remember when it happened. But happen it did.

During my parents' generation, the moment of decision often took place at a church altar with dozens of people kneeling around and praying at the top of their lungs. The scene was loud and boisterous. But when the roar died down into gentle weeping and the occasional honking of runny noses, everyone knew God had received another child into His kingdom.

Today conversions are usually much different. With the help of electronic amplifiers we can still get noisy in the church as we urge people toward the altar. But once they get there, we generally use quieter methods in leading them to salvation. If worshipers sitting in the front pews listen closely, they might overhear the mumbling of an altar counselor gently guiding the seeker toward the door of faith.

Many other seekers are coming to Christ in their homes, with a Bible open and a visitor pointing out the simple steps to salvation.

For many who grew up in the previous generation, when lively altar services were normal, these quieter ways for experiencing conversion often leave them a bit unsure about whether the person really received Christ. If no intense feelings burst through, did anything lasting really happen? Can there be a thorough cleansing of sin and the birth of new life without emotion?

The biblical evidence argues that when it comes to conversion, we should not be too taken up with noise levels and tears. We can't measure conversion with sound-level meters or rain gauges.

When you thumb through the conversion experiences of the New Testament, you will certainly run across a few emotional conversions, like that of Paul on the Damascus road. But by far the greater number of conversions happened when people met Christ in a quiet encounter. Take every one of the 12 disciples, for example.

The Bible's test for conversion focuses not on how loud a person prayed the sinner's prayer but on how lasting was the change in their lives. Did the person make a true about-face in loyalties? Did the person's life-style begin to reflect behavior fitting to a Christian? It was Jesus himself who said, "By their fruit you will recognize them" (Matthew 7:16).

If we get caught up in the habit of connecting conversion with dramatic moments, we may find ourselves holding an empty emotional bag we thought was full of commitment.

But whether enveloped with emotion or not, conversion needs a moment of crisis, a time when we turn from our way to His way.

Probably the most astounding thing about conversion is how dramatic the change can be in such a short time. In a single, brimming instant, a person angry at the world and impossible to live with can be transformed into a happy and joyful human being. Even though this person is still in the same skin, suddenly there is a new creature inside.

American evangelist Dwight L. Moody described it this way: "People had come up to the altar anxious, restless, feeling after God in the darkness; but after conversation and prayer, their faces were filled with joy, and they left not only at peace with God, but filled with joy. And they carried the joy with them to their houses, their jobs, their shops. It could not be hid."

Conversion is a miracle. And nothing proves it quite as clearly as the startling change that happens in an instant of time. A sinner heading in the wrong direction makes the U-turn of life and starts on his way back to God.

Satan's Lie: We're Wiser than God

In conversion stories I've heard there is another common factor. People go away with a new purpose for living. Remember Arthur Miller's best-seller, *Death of a Salesman?* Willy Loman's wife described her husband's blurred sense of direction in these words: "He was a little boat looking for some place to make harbor."

Satan is crafty. He tries to woo us into believing we can navigate our lives better than God can. Why go God's way when we aren't sure where on earth it will take us? Besides, some of the most successful people we know did it "their way." Why give up the good life for some mysterious relation with a Person who might lead us who knows where?

But there's the lie. No matter how brilliant our minds may be, we are so handicapped by sin that we can't possibly choose the best way by ourselves. Conversion places our life goals in the hands of Someone who can refine them and put them in the right order.

God is the One who can salvage collapsed dreams. He brings inner security. He takes a person who feels like a nobody and adds enough meaning to life to make the person feel like a king or queen. That is God's business. And in conversion, a person is only allowing God to perform His specialty—cutting away sin and replacing it with a meaning to life.

Zola Levitt, a Dallas talk show host and author, described how the change in his girlfriend inspired him to try Christ for himself.

Yvonne was a new kind of female for me. She wasn't hungry for anything, she wasn't deceptive. She had no axe to grind. She didn't get excited about all the things secular people got excited about—houses and money and success. At first I thought she was just misinformed, but I finally gathered that she had transcended all that. She was truly above all those things that I was constantly gnashing my teeth over. It was my first experience with a biblically spiritual person. I wanted to try Christ for myself. (*Some of My Best Friends Are Christians,* Regal Books)

More to Come

At least one more thing is true of conversion. It is only the first of many steps. As one man I know of testified, "God has performed a happening in me, and it's still happening."

We have come through a time in the life of the church when we let go of Christians far too soon after their conversion. We helped them come to Christ all right. But then we left them on their own to work out their salvation from there.

Without spiritual roots, and in a climate not suited to Christian life, many wilted to death. We in the church appear wiser now. We have discovered that if Christianity is to take hold in a person and make a difference over the long haul, we have to do a lot of follow-up to the first step.

This follow-up needs two groups of people.

We as veteran Christians must do it. That is the role of spiritual parenting.

But the new converts must do it as well. They must come to grips with the fact that maturing is their responsibility. Coaxing and coaching from others is good. But nothing beats a personal commitment to growth. The first Christians were called "followers of the Way." On purpose they chose to live their lives after the model of Christ, the Way.

For there to be growth, there must first be the creation of life. More than anything else, conversion is that creation of new life in the soul. It is Genesis 1:1, "In the beginning God created," happening all over—one person at a time. But as with the first grand creation, after conversion there is still a good deal of shaping God needs to do.

Joseph Seaborn II is chairman of the Division of Religion and Philosophy at Indiana Wesleyan University, Marion, Ind.

Chapter 2

Entire Sanctification in Plain English

by Jim Edlin

Background Scripture: Leviticus 11:45; 1 Thessalonians 5:23-24; 1 Peter 1:13-25

DOG OWNERS brag a lot about how smart their dogs are. But one dog owner I heard of seemed surprised about his dog's lack of intellect. The man said he had always thought his dog understood every word spoken to him. But just the other day he caught the hound looking up a word in a dictionary.

Maybe the word was "sanctification."

Not many dogs or people use it in everyday conversation. I have never heard a mother tell her child, "Go sanctify your hands before you eat." Small wonder when preachers use the phrase "entire sanctification" few of us respond with a quick mental picture.

Parable of the Secret Closet

One of the best ways to illustrate sanctification is to compare it to housecleaning.

When we invite Jesus into our lives, at conversion, He enters the home of our heart and begins to tidy up room by room. Eventually He comes to a locked closet door. Behind the door are some things we do not want Jesus to see. Perhaps a ball glove, a musical instrument, a gourmet recipe, or the savings account booklet.

These are not bad things, but we would just as soon not have Jesus tamper with them. He might ask us to stop playing ball, since it brings out the worst in our temper. Or He might ask us to volunteer to play the instrument in church. The recipe might generate the same "lose weight" speech the doctor gave us. And who knows what Jesus could ask us to do with our life's savings?

There are other things in the closet too. Of some we are ashamed. We are pretty sure Jesus would not approve of a certain videotape, a feeling we have toward a family member, or the checkbook ledger that shows how we spend our money.

That closet is a warehouse of everything we would rather not have Jesus even know about. And we hold the key to the door. Can we trust Jesus to rearrange and clean out that one last closet of our life? Will we submit to His probing the very depths of our inner selves?

When we hand over the key, Jesus gains complete control of all the rooms of our house. That is entire sanctification.

Sanctification Is Separation

This parable helps us better understand the key idea of entire sanctification, separation. Sanctification basically means we are set apart. Both the Greek and Hebrew words the Bible uses for sanctification convey this idea.

But *from* what are we set apart? And *for* what are we set apart?

Let's take the *for* question first. We are set apart for God and for Him alone. We are reserved for the Lord. Like the priests in ancient Israel, we are used only for His purposes.

The president of the United States has his own personal staff. These people are at his disposal to help him accomplish his many-faceted, world-influencing task. God also has His own personal staff with which He works closely, you and me. There is one important difference, though. When the president's staff goes home at night, they go about their own business. When God's staff goes home, they are still working for Him.

For the sanctified person, all of life is lived for God. At home, work, school, the grocery store, or the ballpark, we are on the job. On the freeway, in the kitchen, over the backyard fence, around town, God's work never stops. There are no vacations or even coffee breaks. Entire sanctification means total involvement in the business of God's kingdom.

If we are set apart totally *for* God, then we are separated *from* anything that is not part of God's program. At the very least, this means sin. Sin is any kind of deliberate, rebellious attitude or action against God. Such things have no place in the life of one completely occupied with God's business.

A little girl who is coloring a homemade birthday card for her mother has no interest in dirtying up her hands, clothes, and hair by making mud pies. She may be tempted to make them if a friend stops by and invites her. But the girl's desire to please her mother, along with her focus on her work, will help her keep out of the mud. The same holds true for the entirely sanctified person.

Yet we have one more thing going for us. That is the working of God within us to help us overcome the temptation. He provides a preference and a power to avoid sin.

This inner resource for the battle against sin is one of the most appealing features of entire sanctification. It gets a lot of press, through preachers, teachers, and writers. There is a great danger in overplaying this feature. It is not a cure-all. The sanctified person is still tempted. An elderly Christian woman once confessed to me she would have never believed the kinds of temptations with which she struggled at her age. Though sanctified for many years, she found her battles with temptation were sometimes severe. I appreciated her honesty.

Satan never tires, and entire sanctification does not insulate us from his attacks. Neither does it throw up a force field that prevents us from wandering into sin. Though God has given us the power to resist, unfortunately the sanctified person may not always tap into this power. When sanctified people do sin, we should seek forgiveness immediately.

The other side of the coin is that the sanctified person should not regularly fall into sin. Instead, we should find ourselves in the habit of obeying the voice of the Spirit and drawing on the power of God. As many people have testified, they find themselves more often the conqueror than the conquered. Entire sanctification means separation from a sinful life-style.

One important question. Just how perfect should a

Christian be? Experience shows that performance can vary from person to person and from situation to situation. Some sanctified folks do not seem very godly at times. Without letting anyone off the hook too easily, we must remember that God sets the standard for each of us individually. If He wanted us to all act the same, He would not have given us different temperaments. Some people are hard-driving go-getters, while others are laid-back flower sniffers.

When Jesus said, "Be perfect, therefore, as your heavenly Father is perfect" (Matthew 5:48), He didn't mean we are to be holy clones, alike in every response to situations in life. The word for "perfect" implies we are to be all God wants us to be today. That is not all we will be tomorrow, nor is it what someone else is today.

One other note on sanctification and separation. Not only are sanctified people set apart from that which is bad in life, but also they can be set apart from things that are good. Life does not allow for everything. And since God's business comes first, we may need to sacrifice some worthwhile activities, possessions, and relationships.

My friend Jun Ooka is a good example. He was a Japanese student of mine when I taught at a seminary in the Philippines. He came from a prosperous family that operated a construction business. He was the only Christian in the family. The rest were Buddhists.

As Jun grew in the faith, he sensed God calling him into ministry. Perhaps missionary service to China. So he left home and came to seminary to prepare for ministry. That is when his family disinherited him. They communicated this by shipping him all his belongings. They wanted to sever all ties.

Fortunately, about a year later, Jun was able to restore this relationship. Though his family remains Buddhist, they have resigned themselves to the fact that Jun will continue preparing for Christian ministry. And they love him anyhow.

Sanctified Oddballs

The result of all this sanctified separation is that it makes you different from other folks. And being different has its drawbacks.

How well do I remember my teen years. My family wasn't poor, but we were certainly conservative financially. We wore clothes till they wore out. But my friends at school were wearing Levi jeans and penny loafers. And I didn't want to stick out like a sore, inappropriately attired thumb. If only I could wear these, I thought, then I would fit in, and I would be happy. Eventually I got my new jeans and shoes.

My attitude has not changed a lot as an adult. I am still not interested in being the odd guy out. Who wants to be the weird one on the block?

But we need to realize that in some ways sanctified people must be different. We have different views and values than non-Christians around us. The books we read, the television shows and videos we watch, the things we spend money on seem strange to many. The way we react to injustice and to our enemies and competitors is about 180 degrees opposite of the way our colleagues react. We don't want to appear weird, but sometimes we may seem that way.

Can you imagine a college professor of physical education preaching to her students that selfless servanthood is more important than winning? Lora Donoho does. She's a phys. ed. prof at Mount Vernon Nazarene College. In a paper she presented at a conference I attended on Christian higher education, she told how entire sanctification affected her work. She said it helped her keep in mind the main message she needed to deliver to her students. That message is selfless servanthood to God. That is radically different from the more common counsel of self-indulgence and winning at any cost.

When Lora talked about her relationship with her students, she told of her desire for community rather than for power and authority. My, my, does she not know anything about how to get ahead in this world? What an unusual teacher.

She is different, of course, not because she wants to be seen as odd. The sanctified person is not different for difference's sake, but for the Kingdom's sake.

Imitating God's Love

The reason we are so different, more than any other reason, is because we are imitating God. This is the goal of entire sanctification. Several times God says in Scripture, "Be holy, because I am holy" (Leviticus 11:45, for example). He is the Pattern for holy living. And we imitate Him. Like Father, like son.

Now how in the world can we be like God? There are a lot of features about God we can never hope to imitate. But there is one we can begin to imitate. It is the feature that is so striking about Him. It is His dominant characteristic: the way He loves.

God loves people who do not love Him. He keeps reaching out to them in spite of their continual rejection. Misunderstood, unappreciated, humiliated, and nailed to a cross, He still loves.

That kind of love is different from this world's version. And those who seek to imitate God will give evidence of that different love.

When I was in the Philippines, a motorcyclist hit the young child of a Filipino woman I know. This lady told me that even she was surprised at her response. Her child did recover but was hurt seriously enough to have to go to a hospital emergency room. Yet in those tense moments after the accident, the woman expressed compassion to the man who had carelessly injured her little one.

In the Filipino culture, people tend to get angry and even violent when someone injures a member of their family.

Physical attacks, or at least verbal ones, are pretty common in situations like this. But by the power of God this woman acted as Jesus would have acted. Because she had an earned reputation for being a fiery person, she not only amazed herself but amazed her neighbors as well.

Sanctification makes a difference. This kind of difference is not a bad thing. It is positive. A life that reacts differently from the hostile way people normally react is the kind of difference our world needs.

Four Key Steps

Let's get practical. How do we come into this experience of entire sanctification? Let me suggest four key steps.

Openness. It all begins with an openness toward God. Honesty is the best policy, especially with God. Why not? He already knows everything anyway. There is no use trying to hide from Him or rationalizing our behavior.

We will never move ahead until we honestly face our predicament. Have we been born again? That is foundational. The life-changing experience of conversion must come first.

Then we must ask how it is going. Do we constantly struggle to do God's will each day? Do we feel like we are fighting an uphill battle with sin? Are there areas of our life that we know are not submitted to God? If that is so, then we need to tell it like it is.

Commitment. Once we know where we stand and admit it, we are moving in the direction of bringing our life before God and giving Him complete control. I suggest a process of committing things to Him one by one.

As a freshman in college I did this in a mental exercise. I visualized myself piling everything I owned on the altar of the church. Before God, I placed my basketball shoes, books, guitar, clothes, and anything else I could think of that seemed important to me. In my mind's eye, I also laid on the altar a rolled-up scroll of blueprints, which represented my ambitions. I added photographs of my girlfriend and other special people whose relationships were important to me. And I threw in a big black trash bag, which stood for all the unknown things that might become so important they could claim control over me.

One by one I mentally brought those things and threw them on the altar in an act of surrender. With some things I hesitated and struggled. Others were easy.

When everything I could think of was lying on the altar, it still seemed like something was missing. It did not take long for God to reveal what it was. I then imagined myself slowly climbing to the top of the heap and lying down before Him. God did not want just my possessions and dreams, He wanted me.

You might say, "I cannot do it. There are some things I just cannot give over to God right now." I understand. In our human frailty we honestly feel we are not able to trust as we would like. There is good news, though. God will help you. We can't separate ourselves for God and from sin on our own power. But we can as God enables us. If you ask Him to help you fully consecrate everything, He will do it.

Rest. When you believe you have turned everything over to God, and there is nothing else you know to do, rest in Him. Sanctification is His job. Your job is simply to commit. He will sanctify. He will set us apart. And He will put His love in our hearts.

So many struggle with knowing whether or not they are entirely sanctified. My advice to them has been: Leave it with God. Be sure there is nothing lacking in your commitment. Then if He sanctifies you right away, fine. If not, fine. Leave it there.

Trust in the knowledge that God is faithful. He said He will sanctify us. He will do what He has promised (1 Thessalonians 5:23-24).

Stay close. We have so much to learn about holy living. And if we are ever to be like God, we must keep as close to Him as possible.

Have you ever noticed how much children are like their parents? It is sometimes shocking to see the way they talk alike, think alike, and act alike. Some say this is a matter of genetics—inherited traits. But my brother's daughter is adopted, yet I notice so many characteristics in her that come from her parents. I would say this is because she spends so much time with them. The more time she spends with them, the more she becomes like them.

So it is with us and God. The more we are with God, the more of His life and love we pick up.

Jim Edlin is assistant professor of biblical literature at MidAmerica Nazarene College, Olathe, Kans.

Chapter 3

Childish Dependency on Feelings

by David A. Seamands

*Background Scripture: Isaiah 30:21; Romans 8:14-16;
1 John 4:1*

THE CHIEF characteristics of toddlers are their total self-centeredness and their inability to wait for anything. Little children demand immediate gratification. They are also almost totally dependent on feelings.

Many adults are babyish in these same ways—self-centered, demanding immediate gratification of desires, and overly dependent on feelings.

Feelings are important, and there is a central place in the Christian religion for the emotional life. The fruit of the Spirit is love, joy, peace, and all three of these include feelings. Christianity in no way relegates the emotions to a second-class status but recognizes that wholeness must include the emotional life. One of the characteristics of life in the Holy Spirit is the free flow of all that is deepest in the human personality. The Spirit frees us to experience and express our emotions.

Feelings and Personality

If you have difficulty with feelings in your general living, you are not going to be a totally changed person emotionally after you are converted or filled with the Spirit.

You will have similar difficulties with feelings in your Christian life. Some people have more trouble along these lines than others do. I think Paul's young disciple, Timothy, was sensitive, prone to depression and discouragement. When he felt low, Paul would have to "stir him up to remembrance" and get him going again.

Some people suffer disillusionment because they believe their Christian experiences should alter their basic personality patterns and temperaments. God is not out to change your personality structure. He can use you to His glory; He wants you just exactly the way you are. In the play *Green Pastures,* Noah in his great moment of acceptance and surrender says, "Lord, I ain't much, but I's all I's got!" That is a very profound statement. The sooner you rejoice in who you really are, the better. For God wants to use you—the unique and irreplaceable you.

We all have problems in certain areas of our lives. As we vary in talents and in gifts, so we vary in our difficulties. However, most people have some problems with their temperament or disposition. Therefore, one of the healthiest things a new Christian can do is to take a good look at himself, accept the basic facts about his personality, and not berate himself because he isn't like someone else.

Our feelings are the most variable and the most unreliable part of our makeup. They are mysterious. They are inexplicable. You cannot directly create a feeling and then command it at will. Feelings are dependent on many factors, some known, some unaccounted for.

The saints of old recognized this. The 16th-century French saint, Fénelon, wrote about "dry spells," those rather feelingless periods in the Christian life. He offered a list of things that can produce these dry moments. Some of the items sound very spiritual, but right in the center of the list is this one: "They also may be caused by well-meaning guests who stay too long in your home." (And you wondered if you were sinful for feeling the same way!) He had the sense to see that feelings are created by a great variety of causes. For example, do you sometimes awaken in the morning in a mood that is completely different from the way you felt the night before? And you can't figure out any good reason for it?

This is why it is so utterly childish to let our feelings control us and, above all, to let them become the thermometer of our spiritual health.

It is only a small step from this control to guilt and resentment and thinking something is wrong with us because we have not had a particular kind of experience or feeling. For then we begin to compare and we "if only," wanting to be someone we're not.

Feelings and Assurance

Some people are dependent on feelings as the basis for their assurance of salvation.

I doubt if any other subject brings as many people to the

pastor as the matter of feelings in relationship to salvation. Because feelings are so variable and unreliable, it is danger- ous to rely on them in this way. This does not mean that the Spirit's witness with my spirit that I am His child will not deeply involve my feelings and emotions, because it cer- tainly will. But feelings must never be made central. They are not meant to take first place in assurance, and if you put them there, you are doomed to be an unhappy and unstable Christian.

This divine order was stated so simply by David, "O taste and see that the Lord is good" (Psalm 34:8, NASB). You cannot reverse that. Experiencing before tasting is im- possible.

The truth of God's promises in Scripture comes first, those promises attested by the life and death and resurrec- tion of Jesus. The truth as seen in the person of Jesus Christ has to be accepted, acted on, submitted to, and believed in before it produces the right feelings. The emphasis in the Bible is on grasping the truth, on establishing the rela- tionship that produces the feelings. That is the divine order. Fact, faith, and feeling. Taste and see—faith, belief, accep- tance, grasping, and then the seeing and the feeling that the Lord is good.

The surest way to become a defeated, morbid, unstable Christian is to always ask yourself, "Well, how do I feel?" To base your relationship to God on the condition of your feel- ings is a certain sign of spiritual babyhood.

The sure road to maturity is to learn to live above moods and feelings. This is going to require discipline. And it will require particular effort for feeling-centered individu- als who have never learned in other areas of life to seek truth before feeling.

I like the suggestion that comes to us from our dear missionary friend from India, Sister Anna Mow. She gives her formula for those blue days when you feel depressed and condemned and are prone to doubt your salvation because you just feel so bad. On those blue days, Anna Mow talks to herself. And that's a good idea. I do that occasionally too, simply because I enjoy intelligent conversation! This is what Anna says to herself when she is not feeling good:

- Did I get enough sleep last night?
- Have I hurt someone, intentionally or inadvertently?
- Do I feel resentment or self-pity?

If all is well in these areas and Anna can find no reason for her spiritual indigestion, she just throws back her head and laughs at herself. And what a wonderfully contagious laugh she has, as she says to herself, "All right, Anna Mow, you stay here in the blues if you want to. I'm going on with the Lord."

There is a profound truth in Anna Mow's simple formula. You are not just your feelings. Your selfhood is above and beyond any feelings you may be having, and you can transcend your feelings. One of the most important steps of growth in the Christian life is to reach the place where you affirm this truth about yourself.

I remember when our son did it. After his senior year in high school, he sold books door-to-door in a distant state. Our phone bill that summer was absolutely phenomenal, because when things weren't right Steve would get on the phone—collect, of course. And we could tell from the first word if he was down. I remember saying to him on the phone again and again, "Steve, you are at the age where you have to face one of the greatest decisions in your life: Are you going to take control of your life and run your feelings? Or are your feelings going to take control of you and run your life?" He went away as a boy. He came back a young man because he made a fundamental decision about himself that summer.

It is a great turning point when you decide you are going to run your life.

The disciples said, "Lord, teach us to pray." Jesus did not answer, "Well, now, when you feel like praying . . ." No. He said, "When you pray, say, 'Our Father.'" You may say,

"But, Lord, I don't feel like saying, 'Our Father.'" It is not Christian merely to say what you feel; it is Christian to say and to pray what you know you ought to feel.

E. Stanley Jones, a Methodist missionary to India, said that sometimes you have to feel yourself into a new way of acting, but at other times you have to act yourself into a new way of feeling.

Faith is basically action. It is belief acted on and lived out that in time produces a certain kind of feeling. That is God's order. Don't try to reverse it, or you will be a childish Christian, unstable in all your ways.

Feelings and Guidance

Many people depend on feelings as the basis for Christian guidance.

One of the great promises of the Christian life is: "For all who are being led by the Spirit of God, these are sons of God" (Romans 8:14, NASB). Nothing is more vital in life than the fact of God's guidance.

But many of us misunderstand this to mean that God always leads us by direct feelings and inner impressions. A common phrase now for guidance is "the hot line to heaven," which means a strong, inner emotional push that may be quite independent of outer influences. Some Christians go to ridiculous lengths on these things, even to the point of praying about what stamp to buy at the post office. I hear of college students who pray about whether they should go to a certain campus activity and then about whether they ought to take a date to the event. I don't know whose prayers are getting answered because a lot of the girls sitting alone in the dorm are praying that the boys will have enough sense to date them.

This perpetual praying for a feeling or an inner voice on what to do runs all the way from the smallest daily decisions to the most serious matters of life. Now the error occurs not about the fact that God does indeed speak through the inner voice. I have had experiences when God did speak that way. The error lies in making feelings and impressions the main source of God's guidance, unchecked and unbalanced with the other, more regular ways in which God guides us.

Feelings and impressions come from three sources: from God, from the devil, and from the inner workings of our minds—our personality patterns, temperament and disposition, emotional hangups and scars, from the damaged emotions of our lives. These are a third source that can be used by either the Holy Spirit or Satan. This is why John warns us, "Beloved, do not believe every spirit, but test the spirits to see whether they are of God" (1 John 4:1, RSV).

A young lady was driving along a country road when she was seized with a strong impression, an overwhelming impulse, that she was to go back and find someone she had passed on the road and witness to him. She was so troubled about it that she came to me for advice. I strongly advised against it; it was obvious to me that there were deep emotional factors in her that Satan was using, not to guide but to misguide. She didn't take the advice but went anyhow. It is a long story filled with incidents both ridiculous and dangerous. All that she accomplished was to bring a bad name on the Lord and on the Christian school where she was a student.

The apostle John's warning means that every subjective Christian experience must be examined and evaluated. It is your moral and spiritual responsibility to test the spirits before you dare to say, "The Lord told me to do this," or, "The Lord led me to do that."

In the everyday decisions of life, you do not need to seek special guidance from God. Many people quote Isaiah 30:21 as the basis for this kind of specific guidance for the daily details of life. "And your ears will hear a word behind you, 'This is the way, walk in it'" (NASB). But by failing to quote the rest of the verse they distort its true meaning. The complete verse goes on to say, "Whenever you turn to the right or to the left." In other words, it is only when you start to get off the track that you will hear the voice saying, "This is the way, walk in it." As long as you are walking in the right path, obeying the directions of the Lord, you may not hear any special voice of guidance, because you do not need it.

If you are a child of God, the Holy Spirit lives in you, you have surrendered your life to Him, you have given Him the controls—then live! Live freely. Live on the assumption that what you are doing is right, because you have power steering: you are led by the Spirit. To stop and expect some feeling or impression on every simple detail of daily life is a vote of no confidence in the Holy Spirit who indwells you and leads you. It is also unnecessary, and one of the surest ways to drive yourself and everybody around you crazy.

In special times of decision when you need a more specific word from God, remember that guidance comes through

- God's Word
- outer circumstances (open and closed doors)
- your own best reasonable thinking
- the counsel of other Christians
- the inner voice of your feelings

These are like five great lights God gives us for guidance. No good ship's captain would just go by one light in the channel. He would crash his ship on the rocks or wreck it on a sandbar. Not even two lights or three lights. The trained navigator lines up all of the lights and then knows he is in the clear, deep channel, and that he can sail safely to his destination.

I remember talking with a missionary pilot just after he had completed a long and difficult course to get his license for instrument flying. After he told me about it, one idea stuck in my mind. He said, "You know, instrument flying is so different from ordinary flying by sight, because you have to learn that you just can't fly by your perception. Sometimes you have to go against your feelings. You just keep your eyes on those instruments. Sometimes you feel as if you are going opposite of what the instruments tell you. You sure can't fly by your feelings."

And you can't fly the Christian flight by your feelings either. Keep your eyes on the instruments: God's Word, the pattern of Christ, the counsel of mature Christian friends, your own best thinking, the outworking of circumstances, and your inner feelings. As much as possible, balance them all together. Put off that childish overdependency on feelings and impressions as the basis for guidance.

Feelings and Good Works

Some people depend on feelings as their motivation for doing good works.

John Wesley, founder of Methodism, preached a devastating sermon in which he warned against "the sin of waiting to feel good before you do good." How often we say, "Well, I just didn't feel like doing it." James wrote, "Whoever knows what is right to do and fails to do it, for him it is sin" (James 4:17, RSV). He did not say, "Whoever knows and feels like doing it."

Like little kids we so often wait on feelings as the basis of our motivation—"Well, I did it because I felt like it." Or, "I didn't do it because I just didn't feel like it." In a world like we live in today—where on every hand we hear and see Jesus Christ in dire need, when we can see Christ poor and naked and hungry and imprisoned—we don't need to feel some special kind of urge to Christian service and good works.

Paul told the Ephesian Christians they were not saved by their good works. We love to quote that part, but we need to go just a little further where he said they were saved unto good works (2:8-10). There are so many unhappy, self-centered Christians who could go a long way toward solving their problems and growing up, if they would quit sitting around taking their spiritual temperature, feeling their emotional pulse, and waiting for some good inner feeling to push them out into the stream of God's service.

To wait to feel good before you do good works is a sin. You can begin now to do some of the good works and services that you know need to be done.

David A. Seamands teaches pastoral ministry at Asbury Theological Seminary in Wilmore, Ky. He is counselor of staff and students there, a former United Methodist pastor, and former missionary to India. This chapter is reprinted by permission from *Putting Away Childish Things,* by David A. Seamands. Published by Victor Books, copyright 1982, SP Publications, Wheaton, Ill.

Chapter 4

How to Live
like a Christian at Work

by Becky Brodin

*Background Scripture: Philippians 2:14-15; Colossians
3:23; 1 Peter 2:12*

THREE A.M. and all's well," I quipped, sliding into my
chair at the nurses' station.

There were only two patients in our cardiac care unit
that night, and both were happily on the mend, leaving us

with a quiet shift. As soon as my notes were updated, I settled in to stare at the monotonous heart rhythms bouncing
across the monitor screens.

The other nurse on duty that night interrupted my
reverie. "Can I talk to you about something?"

Her tone of voice snapped me to attention. "Sure," I
said. "What is it?"

She cleared her throat and began. "I've noticed you
bring your Bible to work every day, and I know you are a
Christian, but . . ." she paused, "as a nurse in this unit you
are dispensable. You have a lot of potential, but the discrep-
ancy between what you could be and what you are is disap-
pointing. Let me give you some advice whether you want it
or not. If I were you I'd become indispensable. Maybe then
someone will listen to your religion."

I was shocked, but I wasn't offended—I knew she was
right. I had learned what I needed in order to get by, but I
hadn't progressed any further. Outside activities had multi-
plied, leaving me a pittance of energy to do a good job at
work. I was eager to share the gospel with my coworkers, but
I'd become blind to the laziness that clouded any chance to
witness effectively.

The next time I worked the day shift, I made an appointment to talk with the head nurse. I apologized for my
laziness and asked her to point out any other attitudes that
hindered the quality of my performance. After that, I apologized to my coworkers, left my Bible at home, and got down
to work.

Our attitudes and actions at work that contradict the
gospel message are costly. Too often we miss the contribution we can make through godly distinctives that set us
apart. These characteristics can cause others to wonder
what makes us different. If our coworkers sense we have
something that they lack, they may be drawn toward Christ.

The apostle Peter calls us to "live such good lives
among the pagans that, though they accuse you of doing

wrong, they may see your good deeds and glorify God on the day he visits us" (1 Peter 2:12). Paul gave Titus a similar challenge: "In all things show yourself to be an example of good deeds, with purity in doctrine, dignified, sound in speech which is beyond reproach, in order that the opponent may be put to shame, having nothing bad to say about us" (Titus 2:7-8, NASB). Even Jesus commanded us to "let your light shine before men, that they may see your good deeds and praise your Father in heaven" (Matthew 5:16). All three passages point out that our behavior does have an effect on others.

Scripture describes four godly distinctives that can set believers apart from the rest of the world. When cultivated, these attitudes and actions can make those watching our lives thirsty to know more.

Work Is Where the Heart Is

The first distinctive is wholeheartedness: When we're at work, we need to be *all* there. If we're in a job God has willed, then we can give that job all we have for His sake. Colossians 3:23 challenges us, "Whatever you do, work at it with all your heart, as working for the Lord, not for men."

Wholeheartedness has a variety of applications, from little things like writing down another person's phone message, refilling the coffeemaker, or returning borrowed files and books, all the way to keeping current professionally, willingly volunteering for extra work, and being an integral, involved employee.

When my coworker confronted me with my poor work habits, I made some changes. Besides leaving my Bible study at home, I started getting up in time to be at work 15 minutes early instead of sliding in under the wire, as my habit had been. I read nursing journals, volunteered to care for difficult patients, and looked for opportunities to lend a hand to my coworkers.

My new wholeheartedness brought benefits in addition to pleasing the Lord. The extra effort increased my enjoyment of the job, and I noticed a growing interest among the other nurses to talk about spiritual topics during downtime.

Your Telltale Tongue

The second characteristic of excellent behavior is discretion in speech. Remember the words to the simple children's song, "Be careful, little tongue, what you say, / For the Father up above is looking down in love"? The Father is not the only one who notices our speech. Those watching our lives also listen carefully to what we say.

Two critical areas of speech either reveal our commitment to Christ or leave others bewildered as to what we believe: the purity of our words and the way we talk about others.

Keeping it clean. After finishing a surgery recently, I was cleaning up when a sackful of bits of suture and paper spilled out on the floor. As I bent over to pick up the strewn pieces, a coworker came over to me. He uttered a couple of swearwords, then smiled at me and said, "Since I knew you wouldn't say that, I've said it for you." It was a small clue he had noticed what was missing from my speech. Abstaining from using the typical array of four-letter words makes Christians remarkably different from their peers.

The same principle governs our jokes. Recently I overheard two nurses joking about one of the doctors who openly identifies himself as a Christian but tells lewd jokes and casually tosses sexual innuendos about. The nurses laughed as they speculated about the range of his duties as an elder at his church. My heart ached when I caught their analysis of the apparent hypocrisy.

There's something out of joint when a professing Christian tells off-color jokes and teases with sexual innuendos.

This sexual bantering is common in our age, but it's inappropriate for us to join in.

Avoiding gossip. Besides abstaining from swearing or off-color jokes, another tricky area is how to handle the bits of gossip that inevitably come my way—they're so easy to pass along. Like all Christians, I need to remember the devastating effects such storytelling can have on relationships. As genuine friendships develop, people begin to exchange personal facts and feelings. Can our coworkers open up to us, knowing we will keep their information confidential? Or have they heard us gossip about others and decided to keep quiet around us? When our speech is free of gossip, we give others a basis for trust.

Service with a Smile

The third godly distinctive that exalts Christ is our willingness to develop and maintain a positive attitude. In the workplace today, everything from the management to the soup of the day offered in the cafeteria are targets for complaint and criticism. Yes, some situations require scrutiny and change. But indulging in unnecessary negativism can become a destructive habit.

Philippians 2:14-15 gives us a different standard: "Do everything without complaining or arguing, so that you may become blameless and pure, children of God without fault in a crooked and depraved generation, in which you shine like stars in the universe." Choosing not to complain in a society of complainers sets us apart.

Every job has its unpopular duties. Where I work, being pulled to another area of the hospital to work triggers grumbling. A coworker answered the phone one day and relayed the message to me that I was being called to work in the surgical preparation area. I responded with a simple, "OK." He did a double take, spun around, and said, "Why don't you whine and complain like everyone else? I've never seen anything like it!" Again, a simple difference in attitude made a statement.

It's especially hard to be positive when we're personally criticized or corrected. It's more natural to become angry and defensive. What will set us apart is choosing to accept criticism and learning from it.

When I was first learning the duties in my present job, another nurse approached me with a slip of paper in hand. She said, "I'm going to criticize your work. There are six or seven things you are not doing right." Then she proceeded to itemize them. I prayed for wisdom, and by God's grace I was able to ask her for more details, to write down her suggestions, and to thank her for her input. Our relationship deepened, instead of splintering because of defensiveness on my part. A month ago this same nurse asked me if I knew of any Bible verses that could help her in a tough situation. There's genuine openness between us.

Swallowing That Pride

The last, and for me the most powerful, characteristic attitude of a Christian in the workplace is the willingness to apologize when wrong. For some unexplainable reason, when we go to those around us and humble ourselves because we've done something wrong, the opportunities to witness open wide.

A while back during the heat of a life-and-death crisis in the operating room, I snapped at another nurse. After things settled down, I went to her and apologized for the manner in which I had spoken to her. She accepted my apology. The next day in the break room, that nurse's best friend approached me. "What makes you so different?" she asked.

I suspected she was referring to my exchange with her friend the day before. "It's because I have a personal relationship with Christ," I responded.

She moved her chair next to mine and began asking

questions. Two days later she approached me again and asked if we could talk outside of work. She confided that she was facing severe personal problems and was looking for someone who could help her deal with them from a spiritual perspective. Nothing else had worked for her. We met at a restaurant and talked for a long while. When I sketched out an illustration of the gospel for her, it made so much sense to her that she bowed her head right there and invited Christ to come into her life.

Had it been worth it to humble myself to her friend? Yes, many times over. In fact, whenever we don't measure up in any of the areas I've discussed, God gives us a second chance if we will humble ourselves:

• If we have become lazy, we can go back and clear the record to allow for another run at working wholeheartedly.

• If our speech falls short, we can apologize to those involved and buy another opportunity to identify with Christ.

• If complaining has encroached on a positive attitude, we can go back and set things right, then rebuild a platform from which to share the gospel.

Although it was painful at the time, I'm glad someone cared enough to tell me about the attitudes and actions that were hampering my witness at work. The investment and effort made in cultivating some godly distinctives in my own work habits has paid off above and beyond what I ever anticipated possible.

Of course, even when our performance and our attitudes begin to reflect the difference Christ makes in our lives, there's no guarantee that our coworkers will be drawn to Him. Godly behavior may make some people uncomfortable and may even subject us to misunderstanding or ridicule.

But there are those who are searching for meaning in the day-to-day routine, who sense in their spirits that there is more to life than just getting by, more to relationships than shared misery and power struggles. To them, a truly Christian attitude is a signpost to a better way. When they see the truth of the gospel in our lives, how natural it will seem for them to accept it from our lips.

Becky Brodin is a former nurse. She currently directs a women's Bible study and evangelism ministry for the Navigators in Colorado Springs.

Chapter 5

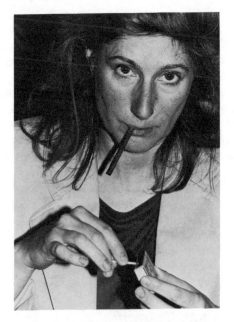

Breaking Habits That Cripple

by David W. Holdren

Background Scripture: 1 Corinthians 10:13; 2 Corinthians 12:9; Ephesians 4:22-24

Habit is a cable; we weave a thread of it every day, and at last we cannot break it."

That's what American educator Horace Mann said in the 1800s.

Fortunately, he was only part right. If we limit ourselves to our own strength, there *are* some habits we can't break. But we don't have to be limited to our own resources. There are other resources and proven techniques available to us.

We don't want to break all our habits, though. Not all of them are bad. Many habits help us. And many others don't seem to make much difference either way.

Consider a few of your habits.

Do you sleep on the same side of the bed each night?

When you shower, shave, brush your teeth, and comb your hair, do you tend to do them in the same order?

Do you have a morning routine related to getting up, getting the newspaper, eating breakfast, letting the dog out, or reading the Bible?

We are all creatures of habit. And some of our habits can cripple our spiritual lives and our relationships with people we love.

Habits That Cripple

As a pastor, I am often faced with the challenge of helping others break the destructive power of habits.

Jack recently got out of the county jail after serving time for driving while intoxicated. The court suspended his license for five years but allowed him early release from jail on the condition he meet me regularly for counseling. Yet even with counseling, Jack's addiction has such a powerful grip on him that he has already slipped a few times and gotten drunk.

Phil is struggling with habits related to pornography and illicit sex. He has sex with prostitutes and masturbates while looking at pornographic magazines and videos.

Steve is a chronic workaholic.

Sharon cannot seem to deal successfully with overeating.

Jim is a fine young man with great potential in medicine, but he struggles with outbursts of destructive temper.

Bob is a new believer with the street savvy that comes from 53 years as a blue-collar businessman in a non-Christian world. He's a painter who owns his own company and who has felt at ease in the rough-and-tumble business world. Though his wife has been a Christian for many years, his past social habits and friendships make him feel uncomfortable with the church crowd. Many of his best friendships have been formed and nurtured in bars, with people not at all like those who surround him in church services. The power of these old habits and friendships is churning up quite a battle for him. He knows the habits are wrong, and the barroom friendships will undermine his relationship with his wife and with God. Yet he feels out of place in church.

These people I shepherd are Christians or desperately want to be. But they are each struggling with chronic, destructive habits.

Here's a sampler of other habits I've discovered can cripple a Christian's spiritual life.

Profanity, coarse language, unwholesome talk

exaggerating, lying, and deception

critical, judgmental attitudes and comments

worry, anxiety, negativism

watching TV video programs that teach worldly values

gossip

tobacco, alcohol, and drug abuse

discourteous driving habits (speeding, angry horn)

overeating

lustful fantasies, flirting, adultery

bad sleep habits (too much or too little)

quick, abusive anger

wasting time, procrastination

Habits That Help

It's not always obvious whether a habit is good or bad. To help us identify healthy habits, I've adapted some clues from Stanton Peele's book *How Much Is Too Much?* (By the way, to identify crippling habits, just consider the opposites of the following list.)

Healthy habits will:

1. Help you feel better about yourself
2. Improve your ability to cope with challenges
3. Enhance physical, mental, and spiritual growth
4. Help improve your relationships with others
5. Bring balance into your life
6. Make allowance for variety and flexibility (not rigidity)
7. Strengthen and empower your Christian witness

A sampler of habits I've observed as healthy for Christians includes the following.

church attendance
tithing
helping others
obeying Christ
putting in an honest day's work
prayer and meditation
Bible study
witnessing

Breaking Bad Habits, Building Good Habits

As Christians, we aren't bound by a lot of rules. We have freedom. But it's responsible freedom. That limits us. It means we're not always free to do as we please, but we have the freedom and power to do what is best for us and for those around us.

Paul addressed this somewhat confusing paradox in 1

Corinthians 6:12 when he said, "'Everything is permissible for me'—but not everything is beneficial. . . . I will not be mastered by anything." He was talking about not being controlled by any custom. But his principle fits perfectly the nature of habits that have the power to control a person. We should be master over our habits, not slaves to them.

Remember the old poem?

> Sow a thought, reap an act;
> Sow an act, reap a habit;
> Sow a habit, reap a destiny.

Gaining control over our habits, and our destiny, can take some time and hard work.

Maybe you can remember testimonies by Christians who said they were instantly delivered from habits like smoking, drinking, or swearing. Steve Miller, editor of this book, tells me his dad, Clyde, was instantly delivered from the smoking habit. After Clyde accepted Christ, he became nauseated every time he tried to smoke. The desire to smoke remained, but the nausea won out.

Maybe something like this has happened to you. Great! God does sometimes instantly deliver people from harmful habits. But it has been my observation that God doesn't usually work that way. He may want to take you through some important lessons and build character through a process of deliverance. Some habits that have deep physical and emotional roots require more extensive "surgery" and healing time.

During my years in pastoral counseling, I've noticed that God usually allows us to break bad habits or make good ones through a process. And the process involves confession, repentance, patience, restitution, discipline, teamwork, dependence, healing, and faith.

I once saw this motto: "Take time to be holy; it takes time." That sure is true when it comes to unlearning and relearning our habits.

Paul gives us a terrific pattern for this process of change. In Ephesians 4:22-24 he advises: "Put off your old self, which is being corrupted by its deceitful desires; . . . be made new in the attitude of your minds; . . . put on the new self, created to be like God in true righteousness and holiness."

How?

Here are some steps I have found helpful and have used in counseling people in my church.

1. Identify areas of need in your life. We have to spot them before we can stop them. To help you do this, think about the opposites on the seven-point list in the section "Habits That Help." (See step 4 in Alcoholics Anonymous' 12 Steps to Recovery, at the end of this chapter.)

2. Stop making excuses for yourself. Quit saying, "That's just me." "I'll never change." "Nobody's perfect." That kind of thinking will doom you to spiritual adolescence.

Start saying, "God is not finished with me yet." "He and I are working on a couple of projects right now." Admit your needs. Confess the bad habits and their damage. Repent of them. (See AA steps 1, 5, 8.)

3. Start someplace specific. Use the rifle shot approach, not the shotgun spray approach. Focus in on one habit. Don't try to change everything. But do start with something, and make it a habit you genuinely believe you can change. Remember, success breeds success. You can deal later with habits that are more challenging.

4. Get help. Commit the need to God. But in addition, seek the help of His Word, His Spirit, and His Church. (See AA steps 2, 6, 11.)

5. Put together a game plan. Outline your strategy in terms of when and how you will begin. Specify your goals for progress. Be patient. Expect some setbacks. But be determined to succeed.

6. Commit yourself to action. Make it a big deal. Pray about the habits you need to break or build. Ask for God's grace and strength. (See AA step 3.)

7. Create a way to make yourself accountable. You can do this in a variety of ways. First, hold yourself accountable to God. But also tell a trusted friend, a counselor, or a pastor about your commitment. Report to this person. Some habits are so embarrassing that you might not want to do this. But this kind of accountability is important, and it's critical in habits that are especially hard to break.

At the very least, keep a personal log or diary. For example, if you are trying to lose weight, climb on the scales every day as one form of accountability. Record your weight and calorie intake as a way of measuring your progress or lack of it.

8. Go for it. Refuse to be mastered by anything except the Spirit of God. And don't give up. Make it a team effort. Your weakness is God's proving ground for His strength.

Paul realized this. That's why he quoted the Lord as saying: "My grace is sufficient for you, for my power is made perfect in weakness" (2 Corinthians 12:9).

And that's why Paul added: "No temptation has seized you except what is common to man. And God is faithful; he will not let you be tempted beyond what you can bear. But when you are tempted, he will also provide a way out so that you can stand up under it" (1 Corinthians 10:13).

So get in touch with the unhealthy habits in your life. Identify the real troublemakers, quit making excuses, and go after them, one at a time. Don't quit. Be relentless. Be surrendered to Christ in the process.

And don't just "weed," but also "feed." Develop and nourish some good habits that encourage physical, emotional, and spiritual growth. Make it a lifelong adventure.

When you do this, your journey to heaven is happier; and it attracts a larger crowd to join you for the trip.

12 Steps to Recovery

Alcoholics Anonymous recommends these 12 steps for overcoming alcohol and drug addiction. They can be helpful steps in overcoming many crippling habits.

1. We admitted we were powerless over chemicals and that our lives had become unmanageable.

2. We came to believe that a power greater than ourselves could restore us to sanity.

3. We made a decision to turn our lives and wills over to God, as we understood Him.

4. We made a searching and fearless moral inventory of ourselves.

5. We admitted to God, to ourselves, and to another human being the exact nature of our wrongs.

6. We were entirely ready to have God remove all these defects of character.

7. We humbly asked Him to remove our shortcomings.

8. We made a list of all persons we had harmed and became willing to make amends to them all.

9. We made direct amends to such people whenever possible except when to do so would injure them or others.

10. We continued to take personal inventory, and when we were wrong, we promptly admitted it.

11. We sought through prayer and meditation to improve our conscious contact with God, as we understood Him, praying only for knowledge of His will for us and the power to carry that out.

12. Having had a spiritual awakening, as a result of these steps, we tried to carry this message to alcoholics, and to practice these principles in all our affairs.

David Holdren is pastor of Cypress Wesleyan Church, Columbus, Ohio.

Chapter 6

Getting Serious About Prayer

by Keith Miller

Background Scripture: Matthew 7:15-23; James 5:16

I PICTURE my inner life as a sort of cavern inside me.

This cavern has a pool of liquid filling it about two-thirds full. The part above the surface of the pool is my conscious life, and the larger part, beneath the surface where I cannot see, is my unconscious life. The day I decided to commit my life completely to God, I scooped up everything I could see above the level of consciousness and offered it to Christ. I felt free; but then, several mornings later a hoary head came up out of the slimy pool, an old resentment.

I was filled with discouragement, and I thought I must not have really committed my life to God at all. But then I realized joyously that of course I had—that all a person does when he commits his "whole life" is to commit that of which he is conscious. And according to many psychologists, the major part of the human psyche is below the level of consciousness.

So the totally "committed" Christian life is a life of continually committing oneself and problems day by day as they are slowly revealed to his own consciousness.

Since I wanted to commit my future to God, I had to find specific ways to align my wavering will to His. I had always "prayed" sporadically; but my prayer life was a rather mechanical monologue. I had prayed about big things (cancer, success, deliverance) but didn't want to disturb God over the little problems of everyday living (resentment, jealousy, laziness). Eventually I realized there are no small decisions —since every decision either takes one closer to or farther from God's will.

To develop a fulfilling prayer life, I had tried books of prayer, reading Psalms, and all sorts of devotional books. But again and again I wound up praying something like: "Dear God, forgive me for all the bad things I do. Help me to be better; thank You for all the many blessings You have given me; and help everybody everywhere." That prayer seemed to pretty well cover everything, but nothing much happened in my life. Then people began to tell me I needed to have a certain period of time each day for private prayer. I tried that . . . and failed, again and again, to get up that few minutes before everyone else did in the mornings.

I can remember the alarm going off those mornings (very early). I would wake up and force myself to feel around in the dark for my robe and slippers in the closet or for my Bible in the blackness. If I couldn't find everything right away, I would tell God sleepily, "Lord, You know it is not fair for me to wake up my family (who need their sleep) just to satisfy my selfish desire to have a time of prayer. Deliver me from that kind of legalism." And I'd go back to bed.

Or I can remember waking up early on cold winter mornings after a late night up and saying, "Lord, You know how unreasonable I am with my family when I don't get enough sleep. And since You made it clear to me recently that I should be more thoughtful of them, I'm going to sleep this morning . . . knowing . . . You will . . . understand."

Or I can remember other times when I have awakened and decided to pray in bed in that semidrowsy, half-conscious state (when the will is disengaged). These times certainly felt "spiritual," but they are not, I learned, to be confused with conscious Christian prayer.

Nothing seemed to be working, and I knew there was something really missing in my prayer life. Finally one day I met a layman whose life had a power and a concern in it that I knew instinctively were the things my Christian life desperately lacked. Everywhere this man went he left in his wake business men and women who began to be different people and whose lives became disciplined and focused on the living God. I asked this man what he considered to be the most important in the discipline of his Christian life. He pointed out that reading the Scriptures every day and having a specific time of prayer for the cultivation of a real and dynamic relationship with Christ were the two things that had become most meaningful and real to him.

Seeing a life with which I could identify did for me what all my "trying" could not—motivated me to begin a regular time of prayer and devotional reading of the Bible each day. I began and, through faith in another man's faith, was able to continue through the dry periods until this time became the center from which I live the rest of my life.

Getting to Know God

At this point things began to change. I realized that if Christianity is a living relationship with God, I had to find out what this God is really like to whom I had committed my future. I realized that my closest relationships had always been with those who knew the most about me and loved me anyway. So I began to reveal my inner life to Him, all of it (even though I knew He already knew). This experience taught me the strange power in prayer of being specific with God. After making as total and complete a confession of all of the moral weaknesses and specific sins I could recall, I thanked Him for His forgiveness. I began to examine myself and "keep current accounts with God."

In trying to be totally honest, I found a new freedom and sense of being accepted. Now I didn't psychologically need to gloss over my true greed and lust and excuse it as being insignificant. I knew I was accepted. Instead of saying, "Lord, today I exaggerated a little on my expense account, but You know everyone does," I was able to say, "Lord, I cheated on my expense account today. Help me not to be a dirty thief." Or instead of saying, "Lord, I couldn't help noticing that secretary down the hall . . . it was such a windy day . . . but, Lord, You know that boys will be boys," I began to be able to level with God and to say openly to him, "Lord, I thought of sleeping with that girl in my imagination. This is the kind of man I am. Forgive me and give me the power and the desire to be different."

As I read the Bible, I began to really believe God would forgive me. Especially convincing is 1 John 1:9: "If we confess our sins, he is faithful and just to forgive us our sins, and to cleanse us from all unrighteousness" (KJV).

The pressures inside my life began to change. In looking

for blessings to thank God for each morning, I began to see His hand everywhere, and life became richer and filled with good things.

For a long time I had been disturbed about the problem of a wandering mind during my time of prayer. I would be trying to pray, and suddenly my mind would jump to a business appointment I needed to make. For years I had forced these thoughts out of my mind to get back to "spiritual things." But now, thanks to another Christian friend, I began to keep a list by my side; and when the thought came to me to call someone, to make an appointment, or to do something for the family, I began to jot it down and then go back to God.

I was at last realizing He is interested in my total life and that these things that came into my mind during prayer might be significant things for me to do. This also made it easier for me to get my mind immediately back to my other prayers.

Sometimes a vision of someone I resented would come floating into my prayers. Instead of suppressing the thought, I began to offer the person to God in prayer, asking Him to make my thoughts about this person more like His. I began to keep a list of people for whom I wanted to pray. And before I knew it, I discovered God was touching more and more of my life through this time of prayer. I realized that the Incarnation means God has made the material world of people and things His concern, and that we must make it our concern for Him.

But there was a fly in the ointment. I found that although I had believed God could forgive me for all my selfishness and sins, I discovered that I could not forgive myself for one of them in particular. After months of inner anguish and continued confession I was talking to a close Christian friend. In a prayer I confessed this sin aloud to God before this friend. And within a few days, I could accept God's forgiveness. As a Protestant I had always been repelled by the idea of confessing my sins before another person. But now I realized why James said, "Confess your sins to one another" (5:16, NASB).

I am not necessarily recommending this to anyone. I am merely saying that I was trapped with some terrible anguish; and through this kind of specific confessing with a trusted friend (whom I knew might fail me), I found myself in a position in which I had to trust God with my reputation . . . and I found a new freedom. I could begin to be more my true self with other people, realizing that as awful as I am, Christ loved me enough to die for me and people like me. Now I really wanted to be different in my life out of gratitude.

A New Honesty

At this point a new honesty crept into my prayers. Before this, I had usually started out by saying, "God, I adore You" (whether I really did or not that morning). Now I could say (when it was true), "Lord, I am sorry, but I am tired of You today. I am tired of trying to do Your will all the time."

But now I could also continue, "But, Lord, forgive me for this: and even though I don't 'feel like' it, I ask You to lead me today to be Your person and to do Your will." This was a real act of faith, because there was no religious feeling involved. My days began to take on the character of adventure.

Howard Butt, Jr., has been a tremendous help to me at this point. He once told me about waking up one morning and beginning a time of prayer only to find that he was as stale and flat as he could be. He couldn't sense God's presence at all. But he said, "God, I thank You for being with me even though I don't feel as if You are within a thousand miles." When he said this, I at once thought it sounded like some kind of autosuggestion; but he continued and said, "Lord, I believe You are here, not because I feel like it, but I believe it on faith in the authority of Your Word. You said

You would be with us." As he continued, I realized that in so much of my life I had been a spiritual sensualist, always wanting to feel God's presence in my prayers and being depressed when I didn't.

I saw that until I could believe without spiritual goose pimples, I would always be vacillating, and my faith would be at the mercy of my feelings. So I tried this praying whether I felt spiritual or not; and for the first time in my life I found that we can live on raw faith. I found that often the very act of praying this way brings later a closer sense of God's presence. And I realized a strange thing: that if a person in his praying has the feeling, he doesn't really need the faith.

I began to feel tender toward God on those mornings during which I would pray without any conscious sense of His presence. I felt this way because at last I was giving back to Him the gift of faith.

A New Behavior

While I was praying for God to reveal His will to me, I was being confronted in my soul with relationships that needed changing: attitudes toward my family, my work, sex, the magazines I was reading, my lack of involvement in politics as a Christian. These and a good many other issues brought me to my knees continually in frustration mixed with the joy of knowing that God was changing my perspective and desires. He was giving me the power to be the free man I had always wanted to be in these areas.

As I continued to pray and read the New Testament, I learned that Christ's criteria for a godly life were not doctrinal as ours so often are. His had to do with allegiance to himself and the fruits that allegiance produced in a person's relationships with other people (John 1:12, NEB; Matthew 7:15-23).

And I began to see that a life of prayer is to be judged not so much by our devotion in praying and witnessing and inner righteousness as by whether or not we have fed the hungry, clothed the naked, and loved the loveless stranger (Matthew 25:31-46).

It dawned on me with a sudden jolt that real prayer, Christian prayer, inevitably drives a person, sooner or later, out of the privacy of his soul, beyond the circle of his little group of Christian friends, and across the barriers between social, racial, and economic strata to find the real closeness of Christ in that involvement with the lives of His lost and groping children, whoever and wherever they may be.

But behind and woven through all of these outer problems and adjustments had developed a new inner prayer life. There was a sense of active adventure. My prayers were no longer vague mystical "feelings." I was communicating with a God who was alive, about real issues and real people in my days and nights. God was trying to give me an abundant new experience of life, when and if I would take it . . . a day and hour at a time. When my regular morning prayers would start out "dry," I learned to read devotional books (like *My Utmost for His Highest,* by Oswald Chambers, or *The Imitation of Christ,* by Thomas à Kempis) to turn my thoughts toward Him, toward Christ.

Then I had found that by following any such reading with a passage from the New Testament every day I was gradually filling my unconscious life with God's message. And as I was revealing myself to Him in confession, He was revealing His character and purposes to me through my rereading the story of how Christ reacted throughout His life, death, and resurrection, and how His Spirit formed and developed the Early Church.

I began to see, as I never had, the relationship of my prayer life to my physical and emotional life. A few minutes of regular exercise or jogging just before prayer time each morning can change the whole climate of one's relationship with God and with other people. Because we are to come to Him with our whole lives, not just our "spirit."

I have learned to love Christ personally. For I have been through years of struggles and failures and joys. I have come to want to find new ways to praise Him for giving me forgiveness and His Spirit, and a sense of wholeness in my life. All of the different personalities I had projected in the various areas of my experience were somehow beginning to be melded into one. I didn't have to have a separate vocabulary, a different kind of humor, and a different set of ethics for my business life, my church life, my family life, and my prayer life. It was as if Christ had taken His fist and begun to knock out the partitions in my soul that had made my life so fragmented.

Finally, I began to see that prayer is not a series of requests to get God to help me do things I think need to be done. Prayer is a direction of life, a focusing of one's most personal and deepest attention Godward. The purpose is to love God and learn to know Him so well that our wills and our actions will be more and more aligned to His, until even our unconscious reactions and purposes will have the mark of His love, His life about them. Prayer was no longer an "activity." It had become the continuing language of that relationship God designed to fulfill a human life.

Keith Miller is an oil entrepreneur-turned-author and public speaker. This chapter is taken from *The Taste of New Wine,* by Keith Miller, 1979 (first published in 1965), Word Books, Dallas. Used by permission.

Chapter 7

The Ups and Downs of Worship

by Don W. Dunnington

Background Scripture: Psalm 100; Romans 12:1-2;
Colossians 3:16-17

REMEMBER THE NEWS STORY a few years ago of the
New Mexico woman who was frying tortillas when she discovered the skillet burns on the bottom of a tortilla resem-
bled the face of Jesus? She was thrilled by her discovery and

showed it to her husband and neighbors. They agreed the marks looked like the face of Jesus.

The woman took this tortilla to her priest and asked him to bless it. She said it had changed her life, and her husband agreed she had become a better wife since her encounter with this unusual tortilla.

The priest was not in the habit of blessing tortillas. The topic had never come up in his seminary training. But he cooperated and pronounced a blessing on it.

Happy, the woman took her tortilla home. She put it in a glass case on a pile of cotton, built an altar for it, and opened a little shrine for visitors. Within a few months, over 8,000 visitors had come to the Shrine of Jesus of the Tortilla. Many agreed the face in the burn marks looked like the face of Jesus. (One reporter, though, said it looked more like the face of a heavyweight boxer.)

It seems incredible to us that anyone would actually worship at a tortilla shrine. Yet in our culture people are worshiping at strange altars and bowing before false gods. Some people are even bowing in church, not realizing they are closer to a nap than to worship. In such a setting, perhaps we need to take a fresh look at what worship is and what it isn't.

Worship, an Ancient Definition

When we publicly worship God in a church, or at a sacred site, or even under a tree, we express our devotion, adoration, and allegiance to Him. We bow before the Lord and acknowledge His mighty work of creation and redemption.

We do this by reading, singing, praying, and retelling the good news of who God is and how by His love we are part of the story of the gospel.

Psalm 100, from the ancient hymnbook of the Hebrews, identifies for us several key elements in worship. This ancient call to worship includes:

thanksgiving: "Enter his gates with thanksgiving" (v. 4).

praise: "And his courts with praise" (v. 4).

joy and **gladness:** "Shout for joy to the Lord . . . Worship the Lord with gladness" (vv. 1-2).

trust and **confidence:** "We are his people" (v. 3).

reverence: "Know that the Lord is God" (v. 3).

What Good Is Worship?

I can think of several ways worship helps us.

It provides the setting for building our faith. When we join with other believers in the public worship of God, our faith is nourished and encouraged by the faith of those around us.

The writer of Hebrews reminds us not to "give up meeting together, as some are in the habit of doing, but let us encourage one another" (10:25).

Martin Luther captured the value of meeting for worship when he wrote: "At home, in my own house, there is no warmth or vigor in me, but in the church when the multitude is gathered together, a fire is kindled in my heart and it breaks its way through."[1]

In worship we begin to identify with the gospel message, and the message continues to change us. As the Word of God is read, preached, and sung and as we share in sacraments, such as the Lord's Supper, our lives are increasingly molded into Christlikeness.

Author Don Saliers observes:

> Worship cultivates the spiritual sensitivity of the individual so that he gradually but surely modifies his ways and makes those adjustments within himself and between himself, others, and God which mark his progress in Christlikeness.[2]

I vividly remember standing in the congregation one Sunday morning singing along with others, when suddenly the words to Fanny Crosby's hymn "Blessed Assurance" laid hold of my soul:

> *Heir of salvation, purchase of God,*
> *Born of His Spirit, washed in His blood!*
> *This is **my** story, this is **my** song,*
> *Praising **my** Savior all the day long.*

In that moment I realized in a fresh way that the good news of the gospel really was "my story." My own personal history has been changed by the grace of God. This flash of insight reminded me of who I am, where I belong, and what my life is about.

Worship gives us the power to overcome the claim of our secular culture that there is nothing more to life than we can see. Focusing our attention on God in the company of other believers strengthens our realization that God really is present in the world. It gives us renewed confidence that there is real meaning in life and that it is found in Jesus Christ.

Worship sanctifies the time in which we live and connects us with Christian people throughout history.

Pitfalls to Avoid in Worship

Public worship is critical to the Christian. It is a discipline we absolutely have to have if we are to mature in Christ. As we participate in it, however, there are some pitfalls we need to avoid.

1. We can go through the motions of worship without really worshiping. On the Sunday morning before I wrote this chapter, our church choir entered the sanctuary and began the service by singing "May Jesus Christ Be Praised."

I faced an important choice. I could choose to let Christ

be praised through my participation in the service, or I could simply go through the motions of worship while my mind roamed from one thing to another.

We longtime Christians are familiar with the worship routine in church. This sometimes works against us.

We know when to stand and when to sit, but we can stand, not out of respect for the Word of God we may be reading, but primarily to stretch our legs.

We can sing hymns without making them our own.

We can listen to others pray but fail to pray ourselves.

We can drop an offering in the plate, but it's more like paying the rent—there is no conscious sense of giving to the Lord.

We can listen to the sermon, but it doesn't seem like God's word to us—at least not today.

How do we avoid this pitfall? We begin by deciding to take part in the worship.

2. We can allow entertainment to substitute for worship. In our spectator-oriented culture we are programmed to watch things happen. We sit back and enjoy performers on the stage, the screen, the playing field.

We judge what is going on according to our likes and dislikes. We don't literally hold up numbers announcing our evaluation of each event: The solo gets a 7. The prayer gets a 6. And the sermon, far too long, gets a 4.

How do we purge this spectator attitude from our worship?

We begin by remembering that worship is not entertainment. In fact, worship is not just what happens on the stage or the platform. It is far more than the activity of the "up-fronters."

It helps if we think of worship as a drama, and every person in the congregation as a member of the cast. God is the audience. What we do, we do in His presence and for His glory.

The people leading the service are prompters, coaching

us as we offer our praise and petitions to the Almighty. The worship leaders are not there to entertain us or to make us feel good. Their primary purpose is to help us all worship God together.

One morning the singing in our college chapel was especially vibrant. A sense of authentic testimony rang out in the joyful music. God was praised. Students and faculty celebrated their victory in Christ.

After the service a student wrote me a note asking why we couldn't have more song services like that. I later explained to him that what happened in the service had little to do with the selection of hymns, the volume of the organ, or the personality of the director. Song services like that usually happen when God's people choose to take part in the worship—when they become part of the drama.

3. We can make the focus of worship more human-centered than God-centered. One of the most common complaints people have about worship services is "I didn't get anything out of it." Perhaps it's because they didn't put anything into it.

There are personal benefits available from our times of worship. I've already mentioned several. But it is important we approach worship not primarily with ourselves and our needs in mind. We come together with other believers to worship God for who He is, not just for what He can do for us.

This pitfall of focusing on ourselves can show up in the songs we sing.

Some songs deal mainly with the experience and emotions of the worshipers. Often these are gospel songs or choruses that tell about what Jesus has done for us or can do for us.

Other songs direct our attention to biblical truths about God's nature and His redemptive activity in Christ.

We have both kinds of songs in our hymnal. And both are helpful in our worship. But as we worship, we need to maintain a balance between what God can do for us and who God is. We are most likely to find the appropriate balance when we choose to worship with both head and heart, with intellect and emotion.

4. We can participate in public worship without leading worshipful lives. The public worship service is where we meet to honor and praise God. We become players in the drama about God's faithful action on behalf of His people. We celebrate the life, death, and resurrection of Jesus Christ. We declare our faith that the Lord is present among us and in our world.

True worship, however, goes beyond what we do in church. True worship extends to worshipful lives. With this in mind, Paul told the Romans: "In view of God's mercy . . . offer your bodies as living sacrifices, holy and pleasing to God—this is your spiritual act of worship" (12:1).

We live worshipful lives when we realize everything we do is done in the presence of the Almighty. And because we want to honor God through our living worship, we do deeds of loving-kindness for others, to the glory of God. In everything we do, we strive to glorify Christ.

Paul said it well:

> Let the word of Christ dwell in you richly as you teach and admonish one another with all wisdom, and as you sing psalms, hymns and spiritual songs with gratitude in your hearts to God. And whatever you do, whether in word or deed, do it all in the name of the Lord Jesus, giving thanks to God the Father through him *(Colossians 3:16-17)*.

True worship is more than what we do in a church building or at the shrine of a burnt tortilla. Worship goes with us into our world when we offer our words, our resources, and our very lives to God as expressions of praise and devotion.

Because of this, we can ask ourselves at the close of each day: Have I worshiped?

1. Douglas Steere, *Prayer and Worship* (New York: Edward W. Hazen Foundation, 1942), 36.
2. Don E. Saliers, *Worship and Spirituality* (Philadelphia: Westminster Press, 1984), 87.

Don Dunnington is chaplain and professor of preaching and pastoral ministry at Trevecca Nazarene College, Nashville.

Chapter 8

Witnessing in a Department Store

by Bonnie Bruno

Background Scripture: Matthew 28:16-20; Acts 1:8-11

KNOWING WHEN TO WITNESS has always been a
problem for me. Oh, I know I'm to carry out my share of the
Great Commission. And I realize that "my life may be the
only Bible someone ever reads."

It's not the how of witnessing that baffles me, but the timing. I want to share the Good News at a good time. I don't want to step on toes and turn people away from the One who can turn their lives around.

One spring afternoon, God must have decided He'd heard enough of my excuses. He sent a boisterous woman across my path to teach me a wonderful lesson about caring.

I was standing at the end of an aisle in a department store, reviewing my shopping list, when I first heard her.

"What crummy weather!" she grumbled to the woman behind the cashier's window. "And to top it off, it's another lousy Monday!"

Her voice was loud enough to attract the attention of shoppers halfway across the store.

"Isn't that flu bug awful?" she went on. Not waiting for an answer, she added, "I'm so tired of sick kids, I could scream."

What a joy she must be to live with, I mused.

I couldn't resist peeking across a row of stationery and pens to get a look at the owner of the shrill voice.

I saw a large woman with stringy hair. Her long, plaid shirttail hung over a pair of baggy jeans. Two little boys huddled inside a shopping cart, pinching and pushing each other when Mama wasn't looking.

A sober-faced cashier counted the woman's cash, then slid it under the window. "Have a nice day, Ma'am."

"Ha!" laughed the woman, tucking the money into a pocket. "It'd take a million dollars to make my day."

She jerked around and slapped her oldest son, about four, across the forearm. "Knock it off, or you'll be sorry!" she snapped. I watched them disappear around the corner into the kitchenware.

How pathetic, I thought, tossing a box of note cards into my empty shopping cart.

You're absolutely right, the Lord seemed to say. So why don't you tell her that I am the only way to happiness?

I couldn't believe what I was hearing. I had felt God's prompting before, but never in a situation like this. I was in the middle of a store filled with rush-hour shoppers. And besides, the woman would probably write me off as a religious fanatic.

I glanced at my watch. It was later than I'd thought. I'd have to hurry if I was going to make it to the library and the post office before they closed.

Are you going to talk to her? God prodded me again.

I swallowed the lump in my throat and sighed. *OK, Lord, but You'll have to bring her to me. I don't have time to run all over the store looking for her.*

I felt a twinge of guilt as I bargained with God. But when I caught a glimpse of the outspoken woman wheeling her cart in the opposite direction, I smiled in relief. Well, that's the end of that, I figured.

But God had another plan—when I least expected it.

I was rounding a corner and heading toward the boys' clothing section when I heard someone shriek, "Give that to me this instant, young man!"

Oh, no.

There was no escape this time. Once again, I felt the Lord tugging at my heart. Now's your opportunity, He seemed to say. You can lighten her load in My name.

Funny, I hadn't thought of it quite that way before. "Lightening someone's load" couldn't be the same as witnessing, could it?

Before I had time to gather my thoughts, the woman was standing beside me, close enough for me to see the beads of sweat on her lip and to smell her stale perfume.

Here I go, Lord, I prayed, almost hoping she'd hurry off again.

"Excuse me," I said, clearing my throat. "I couldn't help

overhear a comment you made to the cashier a few minutes ago."

"Oh, yeah?" She sized me up, then turned away to price the assortment of shampoos. "Your kids got the flu too, huh?"

"Oh, no," I told her. "I mean what you said about needing money."

She squinted and thought for a moment. "Well, I'm always talkin' about bein' broke, so it's hard tellin' what I said." She chuckled and shook her head.

My stomach fluttered. She doesn't even know what I'm talking about, I thought. I'm wasting my breath.

"I heard you telling the cashier that it'd take a million dollars to make you happy," I explained.

"Yeah, you got that right," she said, nodding.

"Well, did you know there's another kind of happiness that can't be bought?"

She eyed me suspiciously but didn't answer.

"It comes from a personal relationship with Jesus Christ," I said.

"Yeah, I've heard that song 'n' dance before." Her eyes darted across the aisle to a tube of hair conditioner.

I went on to describe how very special she was to God, and how a relationship with Jesus was the only key to genuine, lasting happiness.

So what now, Lord? I prayed.

The woman was studying a label, muttering something about the "chemical junk" they added to everything nowadays.

"Well, I hope you'll think about what I've said," I told her.

For a few seconds I could feel my knees trembling. I waited for her to curse at me or tell me to mind my own business.

But her words, quiet and gentle, still echo in my mind.

Tugging self-consciously at her shirttail, she turned and looked me in the eyes.

"Thank you for finding me," she whispered. "I really needed to hear that."

Bonnie Bruno is a free-lance writer in Leesville, La.

Chapter 9

Author Billie Wilson, right, with the Powell family: Bill, Toni, and children, B. J. and Marcia.

When Prayer Wasn't Enough

by Billie Wilson

Background Scripture: Matthew 25:31-46

AS A CHURCH SECRETARY, I've learned that people come first, clerical work second. It was no different the hot autumn day Toni and her baby, Marcia, entered my life.

Our receptionist buzzed my office and said, "There's a young woman here crying. Could you see her?"

Moments later a pretty, dark-haired girl stood in my doorway, a squirmy baby slung on her hip. Soon her story tumbled out.

Unmarried. Broke. Living with the baby's father in a run-down apartment. How had she gotten to this stage in life? Well, the past had always been rough. Parents divorced when she was 2. An absentee dad until the death of her mother when she was 10 years old. Alternately living with her dad and older sister. Choosing wrong friends.

The anguish behind her words grew stronger as she jostled the whimpering baby and said, "I want to be a good mother, but I'm in a mess. When Marcia was born, John* promised to take care of us if I'd live with him. But he works only occasionally and uses the money for drugs. I'm tired of our fights, the crummy apartment and neighborhood. Nothing has worked out. How can I change my life?"

This was going to be a tough one.

"Do you and John talk about your problems?" I said, hunting for words. "That's what my husband and I do when we have difficulty. Maybe the four of us could meet sometime. . . ." A weak beginning I admit, but I'd been caught off guard.

Marcia's whimpers changed to a loud protest. Unable to quiet her with the pacifier, Toni abruptly stood up. "I guess I need to go. She's hungry, and I didn't bring a bottle."

Reluctantly I walked her to the door. "Please come again so that we can talk. I believe God has a purpose in your coming here. He wants to help you."

I couldn't help feeling like a failure that night as I told my husband, Doug, about Toni. I'd heard tragic stories before, but something was different about this one.

"Doug, my inability to help her stuns me as much as her life-style. Do you know what keeps nagging at me? Where would *my* girls be if I'd died when they were 10?"

Instead of dark-eyed Toni, I envisioned one of our daughters weeping in a stranger's office.

Several days later, I went looking for her at her apartment complex. Her description of "crummy" certainly fit the dingy, green buildings. Sagging, open doors said, "No air-conditioning here."

I went door-to-door asking if anyone knew a young woman with a baby. I got no help. My lunch hour was soon over. I prayed as I hurried back to my car. *God, if You want me to help her, please bring her back to my office.*

When Toni Returned

Two days later, she stood at my desk, baby Marcia still on her hip.

"I'm so glad to see you!" I said, jumping up. I tried to hug them, pull up a chair, and take the diaper bag all at the same time.

Smiling, she nestled Marcia in her arms. "I've worked a few days; this was the first chance to come by."

I was still grinning. "I've been praying and even looking for you."

Her dark eyes were somber. "I'm sorry you didn't find me. It's been rough. John and I are miserable. We argue because he loafs at the beach instead of working."

For the next hour she talked about John, her expectations, and their failed relationship. Then it was my turn.

"Remember your question, 'How can I change my life?'" I asked.

She nodded.

"There is an answer for you, Toni." Gently, I explained who Jesus is and the change He had made in my life.

Then I said, "If you want to, you can talk to Jesus right now."

Softly crying, she began to pray: "Jesus, I'm desperate. I've made a mess of my life, and I want to be different. Billie says You're the Son of God, and You died for people like me. I believe it, so please forgive me for all the stuff I've done wrong."

I prayed then. "Father God, thank You for Your faithfulness. You know what has happened. Now please guide and protect Toni and reveal yourself to her."

I looked at the still-bowed head.

"Toni, what are you thinking?"

She smiled at me. "I feel all clean and happy inside. I believe God is giving me a new life."

"You're right," I whispered. "Now you're part of God's family. But think about this: Just as Marcia grows because you feed and care for her, your relationship with Jesus progresses in the same way."

I let that thought sink in, then said, "You need a spiritual mom. Let's meet regularly here."

Eyes shining, she agreed.

I took a deep breath and then continued timidly, "I believe it's important for you to change your relationship with John. You need to marry or else quit living together."

Panicking, she said, "You don't understand. I work part-time in the records department at the hospital. I'm so poor that I have no choice."

"Have you and John ever considered marriage?" I asked.

She shrugged. "Once we did, but now I don't know. I want real commitment and a fresh start. Maybe you and Doug could meet with us. I'll ask him."

But the next morning she appeared in my office, despair clouding her face. "John doesn't love me. We can't get married."

Soon she began to cry. Her words came between the sobs. "I don't know what to do. I have no home and no one to help me except John, and now . . ."

As she talked and wept, I began wrestling with a new idea. Maybe Toni could live with Doug and me.

But I pushed the thought aside. Our talking and crying

ended with my offer to help her find a full-time job and a place to live. Meanwhile, she went back to John.

During the next two days, I telephoned public agencies. Everywhere I found waiting lists, paperwork, and referrals from agency to agency. No immediate help was available.

At the end of the second day I dragged my bag of discouragement home to Doug. Toni couldn't change without help. For several hours we talked, balancing our desire to take her in with the upheaval it would mean to our daughters, 17-year-old Heidi and 23-year-old Wendy.

Finally it came down to this: Would we give her a chance or not? If we didn't, who would?

The next morning, when I told Toni we wanted her and Marcia to live with us, her timid smile affirmed our decision. But that evening, as Doug and I drove to collect her belongings, a cloud of doubts darted around my mind like gnats: John might protest. What if he threatens us? This neighborhood has a reputation for violence.

As we pulled in front of her building, Toni waved from the second-floor landing, obviously watching for us. Trudging up the steps, I tried to ignore the graffiti on the walls.

John was slouched on a dirty, torn sofa. Toni introduced him, and he nodded but didn't speak. I was relieved that his dull-looking eyes showed no resentment toward us.

He watched us carry the few boxes out. Finally Toni said, "Good-bye, John. See you around."

"Yeah," John said, suddenly glaring at her for a moment. Then he turned toward the noisy black-and-white TV.

Live-in Guests

When we arrived home, Toni, Wendy, and Heidi chattered together as they unloaded the car and took turns cuddling Marcia.

Arranging the baby equipment in the freshly cleaned room brought second thoughts: What in the world have we done? We've moved a stranger off the street into our home. She has no references, no way for us to know what kind of person she really is.

I fought the fears with quiet prayer; but the next morning, I confess, I wore more of my real jewelry to work, slipping three leftover pieces under nightgowns in my dresser drawer. I felt I could trust Toni; but what if some of her friends come to visit?

When I came home from the office that evening, I glanced around our family room. A baby bottle and crumpled burp cloth lay on the end table. Toys cluttered the floor. The playpen and swing took the remaining space. How quickly the polished decor had changed.

That wasn't all we had to adjust to. A couple of weeks later, Heidi burst into my bedroom. "Mom, could you *please* ask Toni to take her laundry out of the dryer? I'm tired of doing it for her. While you're at it, give her a cleanup in the kitchen."

I nodded solemnly. "I understand, Honey. But we have to be patient while she settles into a routine. Working nights at the hospital is exhausting, and she was up until two this morning with Marcia's crying. I'm sure she's having a hard time."

Still, I approached Toni, gently reminding her about her laundry. She gave me a startled look and said, "Oh, I forgot. Thanks."

A few evenings later, as I squished our meat loaf ingredients together Toni stood at the stove, stirring Marcia's formula.

"You told me prayer is talking to God," she said. "Now I hear you talking about devotions. What's the difference?"

I gave the meat another thump and turned it into the pan. "I talk to God throughout the day, but for devotions I set aside time to concentrate on Him. Doug and the girls try not to interrupt."

This was new to her.

"What do you *do?*"

"I read the Bible or a devotional book to focus my attention on the Lord. Then I try to listen to Him. Sometimes I share problems or thank Him for an answer or think over a Scripture passage phrase by phrase."

She frowned. "Do you have to do that in the *morning?*"

"No," I said. "Find a time that suits you."

In the days following, I noticed her sitting on the sofa reading her Bible in the late afternoon. Gradually we blended into a whole family. Somewhere between taking turns at the bathroom mirror and playing with Marcia, Wendy and Toni became best friends. Inseparable, they prowled the malls, attended church, and read *The Strong-Willed Child* together.

One afternoon I overheard Toni's exciting announcement to Wendy. "The pastor suggested dedicating Marcia to the Lord right after my baptism next Sunday afternoon. Can you be sure to come?"

At church, a few days later, I glanced around the small group of friends listening to the pastor's encouragement to this single mother. It didn't seem possible she had been with us for three months. As I reflected on her spiritual growth, I thought of the outpouring of God's care and love through many of His people in the church. One friend had helped her make a budget. A midweek Bible study group had repaired her car. A secretary in Doug's office had given Marcia outgrown clothes from her infant granddaughter. Someone had anonymously given $75.00 for Christmas. A dentist had fixed her teeth.

I thought too of the ways in which I had grown because of her. A few days later, we would take another step together in our spiritual walk.

"Good-night, girls," I called to Wendy and Toni as they sprawled on the family room floor. From their open Bible I knew I had interrupted a serious time.

"Mom, join us. We're talking about how we need to have

faith God will give Toni a full-time job at the hospital," Wendy explained.

"I know God has provided for me," Toni said, tears welling up in her eyes, "but I want a dependable income."

Why do these heavy topics always come up when I'm tired and ready for bed? I thought. Still, I sat down with them.

"We know God wants to provide for Toni, but it may be packaged differently. For example, what about a full-time job *outside* the hospital? We'll pray for His continued provision, but let's not limit God by presuming where the job must be."

"I see," Wendy chirped. "Action to go *with* the prayer would be filling out applications at other places too."

Toni nodded.

Two weeks later, she greeted me at the door. "Can you believe I'm now a full-time, bona fide, regular benefits employee at the hospital!"

Whirling me around, she exclaimed, "I begin tomorrow night! God really answered our prayers."

A Fresh Start

Another month passed. More independent and stable, Toni was ready for her own apartment. She and a coworker, another single mother, decided to room together. Friends donated furnishings, and the church gave $750 for utility and rent deposits.

Moving day came too soon. In the midst of boxes and bags, I paused to wipe my tears. "Toni, you're our special daughter. We love you and will always be your family." She returned my hug, promising to visit often.

Her moving out didn't sever the ties we had made over the five months she had lived with us. We still enjoyed watching Marcia gleefully toddle around looking for "Aunt We" (Wendy). And we still helped whenever problems arose.

When Toni's old car died shortly after she bought it, we

placed a notice in our church bulletin. Someone gave her a good four-year-old car. Her circle of friends continued to grow. One day at lunch, Wendy smugly announced, "Toni's dating a guy, Bill Powell, from church. They're a perfect couple."

"That's wonderful!" I exclaimed.

"I want to meet him," Doug stated.

A couple of weeks later Toni bounced into the house holding hands with a muscular, sandy-haired, smiling young man.

His gentle kindness toward Toni immediately impressed me, but Doug tactfully probed for details of his life. He learned Bill had bought a home two years earlier and had worked with his dad to renovate it.

The following month the happy couple returned. Toni waved her hand squealing, "Look at my engagement ring!"

Everyone jumped to hug and congratulate them.

Six weeks blurred in a flurry of wedding activity, and suddenly I sat in the pew listening to the wedding march. Beautifully gowned Toni entered the candlelit church on Doug's arm. At the altar Bill and Toni exchanged wedding vows as I wiped my joyful tears.

Our pastor's words interrupted my reminiscing about Toni's recent journey. "And a special person plays a role in your lives, Bill and Toni. Bill, do you take Marcia to be your child, your responsibility?"

Bill's second "I do" rang out loudly. Marcia lifted her arms to him. Touching his cheek, she whispered "Daddy."

Wiping more tears, I pondered how God had used ordinary people in an ordinary place to change an extraordinary life.

An ecstatic Toni left the altar on Bill's arm, and I remembered her haunting question in my office that long-ago day: "How can I change my life?"

Today she and Bill are parents to Marcia and a baby brother. In our midweek Bible study for young couples, they are regular participants. Toni readily shares her story with unmarried, expectant mothers in our community.

After her son's birth, I visited her in the hospital. During our good-bye hug she whispered, "Billie, I'm the happiest I've ever been in my whole life. Bill is so good to me. I never dreamed I would have the life I have now. I know it's because of Jesus and God's mercy, but thank you for being there for me."

As I left her, Matthew 25:40 came to mind: "Whatever you did for one of the least of these brothers of mine, you did for me."

Maybe Toni would have made it without us, but maybe not. And we wouldn't have known the joy of being God's instruments to change a life. I wouldn't trade that joy for anything.

*John is not his real name.

Billie Wilson and her husband, Doug, live in Titusville, Fla.

Chapter 10

Priorities:
The Battle for First Place

by Charles R. Swindoll

Background Scripture: Matthew 6:33; Luke 14:15-24;
Colossians 1:13-18

LIFE places before us hundreds of possibilities. Some are bad. Many are good. A few, the best. But each of us must decide, "What priority takes first place in my life?"

We aren't left with many options. Jesus himself gave us the top priority. "But seek first His kingdom and His righteousness; and all these things shall be added to you" (Matthew 6:33).[1] He said, in effect, "This is your priority; this comes first." He even uses the words "But seek *first*."

Frankly, we don't even have to pray about our top priority. We just have to know what it is, then do it. If I am to seek first in my life God's kingdom and God's righteousness, then whatever else I do ought to relate to that goal: where I work, with whom I spend my time, the one I marry, or the decision to remain single. Every decision I make ought to be run through the Matthew 6:33 filter.

The Important Things Are Invisible

I'll never forget a talk I had with the late Corrie ten Boom. She said to me, in her broken English, "Chuck, I've learned that we must hold everything loosely, because when I grip it tightly, it hurts when the Father pries my fingers loose and takes it from me!" Things of significant value are the unseen things, aren't they? But that is easy to forget.

I have a friend who, in midcareer, was called into the ministry. In fact, God ultimately led him overseas. At that point he found it necessary to move all his family and as many of their possessions as possible beyond these shores, all the way to the island of Okinawa. He told me, "We packed everything we could in barrels and shipped them on ahead. And then we put all of our possessions that were a part of our trip into our station wagon. We packed that car all the way to the top of the windows."

While driving to the place where they would meet the ship that would take them to the Orient, they stopped for a rest and a bite to eat. While they were inside the restaurant, a thief broke into their station wagon and took *everything* except the car. Nice of him to leave the car, wasn't it? "The only thing we had," he said, "were the articles of clothing on our backs. Our hearts sank to the bottom!" When asked about it later, he said, "Well, I had to face the fact that I was holding real tight to the things in that car. And the Lord simply turned my hands over and gave them a slap . . . and out came everything that was in that car. And it all became a part of the Father's possession."

What tangibles are you holding onto? Have they become your security? Are you a slave to some image? Some name you're trying to live up to? Some job? Some possession? Some person? Some goal? (Nothing wrong with having goals; but something is wrong when they have you in their grip.) Let me give you a tip. If you cannot let it go, it's a priority to you. It is impossible to be a slave to things or people and at the same time be a faithful servant of God.

Now before we let this idea of "letting go" appear too stark, look again at the wonderful promise in verse 33. The latter half of it says, "all these things shall be added to you." How interesting! Remember verse 32—"these things the Gentiles eagerly seek"? Well, now Jesus is saying "these things shall be added to you." Those who seek them are off target. But those who seek Him are provided with whatever they need. When you think all that through, it just depends on where your priorities are. Isn't that a relief? Once you have given them to the Lord, who knows, He may turn right around and let you enjoy an abundance. Or He may keep them from you at a safe distance and just every once in a while let you enjoy a few. But they'll all be added to you from His hand rather than from your own.

You may be able to identify with the man who wrote these words:

> I am 42 years old. I work for a large corporation. But I'm no longer moving "up."
>
> I know that working for a large corporation is not exactly *au courant,* but my father owned a small retail

store, and after 30 years of his standing behind the counter, neither of us saw the magic of doing "your own thing."

But a big corporation—something plucked right off the Fortune 500; a company with interlocking, multinational profit centers; with well-defined vertical and horizontal reporting relationships—that was just what the doctor ordered, and that was exactly what I got.

Going in, I knew there would be a price to pay. Too much structure can be confining. But for me, the organizational chart was like a children's playground—a place to climb, swing, and scramble all the way to the top.

And that was where I was headed. After all, isn't that what it's all about?

Year by year, level by level, I made my way up; and if I wasn't laughing all the way, only rarely did I doubt choosing the corporate life.

Never being one for team sports, never having served in the army, I enjoyed the camaraderie that comes from being "one of the boys."

I also enjoyed the competition.

Whatever the reason . . . I was immediately perceived to be "a star." And though my corporation was too conservative to have a "fast track," I did burn a few cinders as a steady procession of blue memos charted my upward progress. Over the years I gained titles, windows, salary, and perks. These incentives fueled a fire that was burning very bright indeed. I knew in my bones that I would someday reach the top. Some men might stumble. Others might even fall by the wayside. But not me; never me.

Or so I believed, right up to the day, right up to the instant, when I learned the fire was out, the star was extinguished, the climb was over. . . .

. . . I could expect the average increases due the average employee. But there would be no more leapfrog advancements. No more seductive little perks. No more blue memos.

I was no longer climbing. I had plateaued out. . . .[2]

No doubt, this man felt the same sense of loss that my missionary friend experienced when he said, "The Lord simply turned my hands over . . . gave them a good slap . . . and out came everything!"

Now I wouldn't wish that jolt on anyone, but it happens to many. If your career, however, is simply a part of God's plan and you keep it in proper perspective, you can handle a demotion just as well as you can handle a promotion. It all depends on who's first.

Who's on First?

There is a line in the Jewish Talmud that goes like this: "Man is born with his hands clenched; he dies with them wide open. Entering life, he desires to grasp everything; leaving the world, all he possessed has slipped away."

A few words from Colossians 1 never fail to encourage me when possessions begin to slip away. Since life is like a coin and it can be spent only once, these words are good reminders of the One deserving of our investment. They begin with a reference to God the Father:

> For He delivered us from the domain of darkness, and transferred us to the kingdom of His beloved Son, in whom we have redemption, the forgiveness of sins *(vv. 13-14)*.

That is a wonderful statement of God's eternal rescue. He delivered us from darkness to light. And He transferred us to a new kingdom—the unseen kingdom—where there are values worth investing in, where we live beyond the entrapment of things and people and events and human ideas. It is called "the kingdom of His beloved Son [Jesus Christ]." He has transferred us to a new realm of existence where we are enveloped in the Son's perfect righteousness and forgiveness.

And what a statement follows!

> And He is the image of the invisible God, the first-born of all creation. For by Him all things were created, both in the heavens and on earth, visible and invisible, whether thrones or dominions or rulers or authorities—all things have been created by Him and for Him *(vv. 15-16)*.

Everything created was through Christ and His power, and furthermore, it was created for His honor. That includes everyday things today. You have a good job? It's to be enjoyed for Him. You have a nice salary? It's to be enjoyed and invested for Him. You have good health? It is for Him. You have a family? The family members are for Him. You're planning a move? It's to be for Him. You're thinking about a career change? It needs to be for Him.

> And He is before all things, and in Him all things hold together *(v. 17)*.

Isn't this a wonderful section of Scripture? In all these things, Christ is the center. He is in things, He's through things, He's holding things together. He's the glue that makes stuff stick together. He put the stars in space, and their movement is exactly according to His sovereign chronometer, precisely as He arranged it. And everything out there hangs in space exactly as He set it up. His problem is not with planets in space, however. His wrestling match is with people on earth who have been put here but want to go their own way. Note the next verse:

> He is also head of the body, the church; and He is the beginning, the first-born from the dead; so that He Himself might come to have first place in everything *(v. 18)*.

Take your time with those final four words. Read them aloud. Think them through. You're dating a young man. You think you're falling in love with this man. Does Christ have *first place* in that relationship? Or have you decided that a moral compromise really feels better? Maybe you have chosen not to maintain such a strict standard of purity as before. If you've made that priority decision, then face it— Christ really isn't in first place in that romance.

Why am I coming on so strong? Because He is to have *first place* in everything. Those who are really committed to excellence give Him top priority.

A Story About Priorities

On one occasion Jesus was having a meal with a group of people. When the other guests began picking out places of honor at the table, Jesus told them a story about humility. And to the host he said:

"... when you give a reception, invite the poor, the crippled, the lame, the blind, and you will be blessed, since they do not have the means to repay you...."

And when one of those who were reclining at the table with Him heard this, he said to Him, "Blessed is everyone who shall eat bread in the kingdom of God!" *(Luke 14:13-15)*.

Someone else says this to Jesus. The light finally dawned. He's gotten the message! "Lord, I've heard what You have said and it's clear that the one who is really fulfilled, deeply satisfied, genuinely joyful, is the one who enjoys Your food, who takes Your provisions, and lives in light of them while he's on this earth. I believe that, Lord. Count me in!" That's the general idea.

Jesus heard his response and told another story that illustrates everything I have been trying to say in this chapter.

But He said to him, "A certain man was giving a big

dinner, and he invited many; and at the dinner hour he sent his slave to say to those who had been invited, 'Come; for everything is ready now'" *(Luke 14:16-17)*.

But wait. This isn't a literal meal He's talking about. This is a parable, remember? He is talking about a spiritual meal—that which satisfies one's life in the kingdom realm. He's saying, "I've served a meal, and it will satisfy you. Come and eat." You'd think everybody would have jumped up and joined in. Not so.

> "But they all alike began to make excuses. The first one said to him, 'I have bought a piece of land and I need to go out and look at it; please consider me excused'" *(Luke 14:18)*.

Here is a guy who has made an investment. Like many, he has bought a piece of land. If you've ever bought a piece of land, you know there's nothing quite as encouraging as walking across the dirt. You want to sort of dig your toes in it. "It's mine! . . . My land! My piece of property! I own this!" You see, he was preoccupied with his purchase. He planned to accept the master's invitation, but he thought he would come later. "Right now I want to look over my investment. Please consider me excused. My purchase comes first."

Nazarene sociologist Jon Johnston pulled no punches when he wrote:

> Self-denial is the perennial challenge of humanity. A rampant selfishness is omnipresent in every generation, and the church . . . is not immune to me-ism. In fact, many declare our Zion has opted for a double dose. Clergy and parishioner alike calculate every move to maximize personal benefit. . . .
>
> Today, our bonfires of selfishness are fueled by the gasoline of affluence. . . .
>
> Today's self-centered churchgoer asks the same question of God, coupled with another one: "What will you do

for me soon?" God is pictured as the dispenser (and with-
holder) of life's prizes—a television game-show host.
. . . We conclude that such things as good health, fortune, and success are sure indicators of his approval for
our lives. This is the Protestant ethic gone to seed. . . ."[3]

But let's get back to Jesus' story and see how others
responded to the dinner invitation.

"And another one said, 'I have bought five yoke of
oxen, and I am going to try them out; please consider me
excused'" *(Luke 14:19).*

Most of us don't buy oxen today. We buy a lot of other
things, though. Whatever we buy, we love to try out. We like
to take care of it. We like to shine it. We like to look at it.
Deep down inside we tend to make a little shrine out of it,
because we worked so hard for it and it means so much. This
guest is doing that. He's saying, "I've got this possession and
I want to try it out. Please consider me excused."

I am especially intrigued at the third person's excuse.
Look at what this guy has to say:

"And another one said, 'I have married a wife, and for
that reason I cannot come'" *(Luke 14:20).*

"Lord, come on. Gimme a break. At least wait till after
the honeymoon. You know, give me a little time. I'll be there
later, I promise; but right now there is a relationship that
keeps me from coming to Your meal."

Not one of these things is wrong in and of itself. There
is nothing wrong with land. Nothing wrong with oxen. Nothing wrong with marriage. So what's wrong then? Well, as
good as they are, they prevented these three individuals
from being satisfied with the priority of eating a kingdom
meal. They took first place, that's all. But that's EVERY-
THING . . . really, that's EVERYTHING! And that is precisely Jesus' point.

New Testament scholar William Barclay writes,

It's possible to be a follower of Jesus without being a disciple; to be a camp-follower without being a soldier of the king; to be a hanger-on in some great work without pulling one's weight. Once someone was talking to a great scholar about a younger man. He said, "So and so tells me that he was one of your students." The teacher answered devastatingly, "He may have attended my lectures, but he was not one of my students." There is a world of difference between attending lectures and being a student. It is one of the supreme handicaps of the Church that in the Church there are so many distant followers of Jesus and so few real disciples.[4]

I think the ranks were thinned. I think Jesus decided, "I don't want a big crowd following Me if it means that all these people want to do is feed their bellies and watch miracles and listen to My stories and passively respond to lectures. I want those who give Me top priority."

If I stated to you in one succinct sentence the message of this chapter, it would be: Whatever is in first place, if it isn't Christ alone, it is in the wrong place. Life is a lot like a coin; you can spend it any way you wish, but you can spend it only once. What are you spending it on? What is really first in your life?

---

1. All Bible references are from the *New American Standard Bible.*

2. Robert Goldman, "Getting Stuck on the Way Up the Corporate Ladder," *Wall Street Journal,* January 6, 1986.

3. Jon Johnston, "Growing Me-ism and Materialism," *Christianity Today,* January 17, 1986, 16-I. Copyright © 1986 by Christianity Today, Inc., Carol Stream, Ill.

4. William Barclay, *The Gospel of Luke, The Daily Study Bible* (Edinburgh: Saint Andrew Press), 203.

Charles R. Swindoll is pastor of First Evangelical Free Church of Fullerton, Calif., and author of many books. This chapter is reprinted by permission from *Living Above the Level of Mediocrity: A Commitment to Excellence,* by Charles Swindoll, copyright © 1987 by Charles R. Swindoll. Published by Word Books, Waco, Tex.

Chapter 11

Tapping into
Attitude Power

by Nina E. Beegle

Background Scripture: 1 Corinthians 13:11; Philippians 4:8; Colossians 3:10-14

I LEARNED my most memorable lesson about attitudes from Mrs. Erskine. She went to church where I did. Her husband was a retired minister, and they were both getting up in years, but they took in foster children.

One afternoon she came to the women's meeting with a new little charge, less than a month old. I laid my own tiny twins on the bed beside him and propped coats and pillows around them. As I did, I noticed the foster baby was not very responsive, and his eyes rolled strangely.

Under Mrs. Erskine's loving care the baby grew physically, but he never walked. Neither did he talk. They laid him on the pew during church, and there he was content to remain, long after other children his age would have been squirming and exploring. His guttural sounds during church services never elicited a flicker of impatience or embarrassment from the Erskines.

Finally, he grew to three, then four feet in length. It was obvious he came from hardy stock, and he was dead weight to carry. But Mrs. Erskine lovingly carried him wherever she went. As she carried him from the sanctuary one Sunday morning, I greeted her in the foyer.

"That boy is getting to be quite a heavy burden for you, isn't he, Mrs. Erskine?"

I'll never forget her response. She looked at me and quietly replied, "Our burdens are only as heavy as our attitudes make them."

Every once in a while those words come back to me like an echo when I begin to strain under some weighty load in my own life.

We cannot always control our circumstances, but we can learn to control our attitudes.

Attitude Control in Auschwitz

Dr. Victor Frankl, a German psychiatrist, endured several years of heartbreaking pain and indignity during the Holocaust. Hitler's solution to the Jewish "problem" had already slaughtered Frankl's entire family, young children and all. Of Frankl's immediate family, only he and one sister were left.

With all but his sister gone, the Nazis shipped Frankl from the concentration camp at Dachau to the one at Auschwitz. They had taken his family, his freedom, and his possessions. They shaved his head, took his clothes, and gave him prison garb.

There was one thing they could not take away, though. He survived to describe it in his book, *Man's Search for Meaning:* "The last of the human freedoms—to choose one's attitude in any given set of circumstances." Surrounded by dying inmates, and controlled by a people who did not want to waste bullets on Jews, Frankl chose to endure with dignity.

An attitude, the dictionaries say, is a thought process that affects the way we feel and act. We weren't born with the attitudes we now have. We grew them over the years. We fed them on our educational, social, and religious experiences. During that growing process, attitudes can change radically.

That's what happened with Anne Sullivan, the woman who taught the blind, deaf, and mute Helen Keller. Most people know a bit about Keller's achievements in overcoming her handicap. But few know about the turnaround in Anne's attitude that would later help Keller break out of her shell.

Anne's childhood was in some ways a greater obstacle to achievement than Keller's. At least Keller had the advantage of parents who loved her, and the security that accompanies that love. Anne's childhood was filled with the kind of hardships that can churn up bitterness and crippling self-pity.

As a young girl, an eye disease left her partially blind. Before she was eight, her mother died from tuberculosis. She was left to keep house for her abusive, alcoholic father. Her brother and sister had gone to live with their father's brother. When this uncle learned that Anne's father was beating and abusing her badly, he took her to his home also.

His wife, however, later sent Anne to Tewksbury, an institution Anne's uncle described as a place for "the sick, the insane, the criminals, the defeated, the lowest scum." But he could not change his wife's mind. She insisted Anne was a bad influence on their own children. This woman also sent Anne's little brother Jimmie, who died in the awful place within three months.

After three years at Tewksbury, Anne was sent to an institution for the blind. At age 13 she still could not read. The other children ridiculed her for that. But the matron of the school noticed the unfortunate girl and began helping and encouraging her. She even took Anne to her Cape Cod home during a vacation period and taught her to swim.

With the help of this matron, Anne's attitude began to change. She began to work hard at her studies. She graduated as the valedictorian of her class. Her valedictory speech was prophetic of her own life. The last two paragraphs read:

"And now we are going out into the busy world to take our share in life's burdens, and do our little to make the world better, wiser, and happier.

"Fellow graduates, duty bids us go forth into an active life. Let us go cheerfully, hopefully, and earnestly and set ourselves to find our special part. When we have found it, willingly and faithfully perform it; for every obstacle we overcome, every success we achieve tends to bring man closer to God and makes life more as He would have it."

We Are What We Think

As a man "thinks within himself, so he is" (Proverbs 23:7, NASB). That suggests we become what we allow our thoughts or attitudes to make us. Because attitudes can come to life in words and behavior, there is power behind them.

It's not a power that has to control us. Instead, we can control it. We can accept our attitudes or reject them—put them on or take them off as we would a coat. We need not be victimized by them.

That's the message Paul gave to the Philippians when, in 4:8 (NASB), he told the people to think on whatever is true, honorable, right, pure, lovely, of good repute, of excellence, and worthy of praise. In other words, we should cultivate positive attitudes, not negative ones. For example, when we find ourselves mentally telling off our boss or spouse in an imaginary conversation, we should eject those thoughts from our brain the moment we realize what we're doing.

Negative thoughts like these can destroy us and others, spiritually and physically. But positive thoughts can bless us and others. A woman I know describes her life's philosophy as "a determined pursuit of joy." Her vibrant enthusiasm for life is expressed in service to others. "To find joy," she says, "one must observe it, seek it, and give it."

How to Change an Attitude

You don't usually change an attitude overnight. The Bible describes changes in attitude with phrases like "put on," "put off," and "put behind me" (Colossians 3:10-14; Ephesians 4:22-24; 1 Corinthians 13:11). This "putting process" often takes time.

Some change happens instantaneously, though, like the flash of revelation that prompts it. What happens in the truly "born again" experience is an inexplicable, cataclysmic change—a phenomenon so pervasive and inclusive that it swallows up understanding and reason. The about-face just doesn't make sense to observers who watch the change. Though rebirth involves an act of the will, it does what the

person himself cannot do and often surprises its very subject.

Rebirth changes some attitudes instantly: What I hated
I suddenly love. In the twinkling of an eye my thoughts,
which all revolved around myself, now revolve around others: their eternal destiny, their feelings, their needs.

Many attitudes, however, change more slowly. The
putting off the old, the putting on the new, and the putting
away of childish things become the ongoing work of the Holy
Spirit. There are so many bad attitudes to "put off" before
we can start "putting on" good ones.

Take, for instance, a young man I know. I'll call him
Eric. He had just accepted Christ into his life, but he was
having a profound struggle in his marriage.

He told me about some of the problems he was having
with his wife. Then he added, "I just don't have any more
feeling for her. What I once felt is dead."

Cruel words and retaliation had built giant walls between the two and the romance they once enjoyed. Reconcil-
iation seemed impossible, even to me. But I sent up a prayer
for help.

"Eric," I said before he left, "could you, no matter how
you feel, begin to treat her as though nothing had gone
wrong in your marriage? I know it wouldn't be easy, and you
couldn't expect instant results. But could you come up behind her while she's washing dishes and put your arm
around her and tell her how good the dinner was?"

I suggested other things that, from my woman's point of
view, I felt would make her responsive to him. (She wasn't
exactly a shrew.) He didn't know if he could do anything so
drastic, but he said he would try.

Magic happened.

When Eric phoned to tell me about it, he said, "It's
working. She's a different person, and I'm feeling a lot different toward her."

True, we had put the cart before the horse, but it got the

cart moving. Attitudes are supposed to change behavior, but in this case the behavior came first, then the attitudes changed.

Some of us have traveled with a certain negative attitude for so long we've worn ourselves into a rut. It's like we're driving in a deep ditch. We try to drive up the bank and out of the ditch, but we end up spinning our wheels and watching the dirt fly. In cases like this we may need a tow—outside human help.

Sharing the problem with a trusted friend, pastor, or counselor may help us more objectively examine our attitude, pray over it, and change it.

Attitudes in the Church

You would think that since Christ is the Head of the Church that people would find within its fellowship more kindness, love, and compassion than anywhere else. It has been my experience that this is generally the case. However, I know some who say people in the church have treated them worse than any other human beings have. That, too, has been my experience.

Why?

Perhaps it is because there are, and ought to be, people within each church body who are not Christians. Second, there are some who are not believers even though they profess to be. Third, the archenemy of the Church makes it his battle arena. These three factors considered, and added to the frail humanity of true believers, we have to expect destructive attitudes within the fellowship.

Undoubtedly, the most damage comes from people in the second group: the pretend pious. Though Jesus showed great compassion for most sinners, He was scathing and relentless in attacking godless men who claimed to be godly. He used terms like: "hypocrites," "white-washed tombs full of dead men's bones," "your father the devil," "stiff-necked and uncircumcised," "stumbling blocks," "blind guides," "vipers."

Descendants of these people are still in the church today, like the amaranth with its drooping, crimson flower cluster, hiding its weedship. This plant looks attractive at first glance. But a closer look reveals why it is related to pigweed and tumbleweed. It flourishes in the grain field and garden, stealing nourishment from the healthy plants.

So our unregenerate professors of religion do their damage. Yet Jesus said we should not try to sort them out. We are to let the wheat and the weeds grow together. The weeding is God's job, and He will take care of it in due time.

So, since we, the Church, are relieved of the responsibility for sorting them out, we must learn how best to tolerate them so that they'll do the least damage. Jesus gave some guidelines for that. We could call them the Be-attitudes.

Be meek, merciful, pure in heart, peacemakers. You can read about these virtues and others in Matthew 5:1-10. If our attitudes can embrace these virtues, we can find freedom from the hostile attitudes we've learned from the past. And we can find the power to maintain control over our attitudes in the face of adversity. If Victor Frankl could tap into this power in a Nazi concentration camp, we can do it, too, where we live.

The bad news is that with the thoughts we concentrate on, and the attitudes that develop, we can paint gloomy clouds over our lives.

But the good news is we can allow our thoughts to become brush strokes that add rainbows to our lives.

Nina Beegle is a free-lance writer and the wife of a Free Methodist pastor in Canon City, Colo.

Chapter 12

Restoring the Spiritual Zest

by Ann Cubie Rearick

Background Scripture: Matthew 13:1-23; Philemon 6;
Revelation 2:1-7

IT TOOK THE DEATH of my baby brother on the streets of the city for me to once again have a vital relationship with Christ."

Those are the words of a friend of mine, now a vibrant

Christian woman. Her brother was in his early 20s when a gunman shot him down on the streets of Miami.

My friend was not living a dynamic Christian life when her brother was killed. She attended church more often than not, but she was at a low ebb in her spiritual life. If her faith were an ocean, it was at low tide.

Serving Christ had become secondary to the other responsibilities of life. However, in the midst of grief she turned to the One who could help her, and renewal came.

Why Do We Lose Our Zest?

I don't know how my friend managed to ease Christ into a lesser role in her life. But I do know a lot of Christians do just that. That's the unhappy news. The happy news is it doesn't need to take a tragedy to get us back on track.

I believe there are well-meaning Christians in every church for whom being a Christian has become a habit rather than a living faith. These people may regularly attend church, take on the church chores expected of them, and perhaps even serve in top positions of leadership. But they have no joy, none of the abundant life Jesus said He came to bring.

The problem is not new. Jesus dealt with this very issue when He told the parable of the farmer sowing seed (Matthew 13:1-23). He talked about thorns that grew up and choked the plants. Actually, He wasn't talking about thorns and plants. He was talking about the worries of this life choking to death our spiritual vitality.

We know sin will separate us from God. But Jesus was talking about how everyday affairs of life can also separate us from the Lord. We all occasionally have to grapple with problems and worries. Difficulties at work, with the children, in the community, at school—these are common to us all.

But if we let our minds focus constantly on the problems, and not on the One who can help us overcome them, our spiritual vitality and joy can die a slow, choking death. Sadly, there are those sitting in church pews to whom this has happened. These are worshipers who wonder why the services seem dry and God seems so far away.

Good-bye, First Love

Perhaps this is what happened to the men and women in the church at Ephesus. In Christ's message to the church recorded in Revelation 2:1-7, He commended the people for their good deeds, their hard work, and their perseverance. He also recognized their diligent stand against wickedness and false beliefs of the day.

But then comes the tragic statement: "I hold this against you: You have forsaken your first love" (v. 4).

They were following the routine, living out their religious habit. But the spiritual life was gone.

Christ warned the church not to chastise them but to call them back to their "first love," the love that makes serving Christ a joy.

We don't know how the Ephesians responded. But I do know there are many Christians today who are rediscovering their first love.

What It Takes
to Restore the Zest

Sometimes renewal comes in the aftermath of tragedy, like my friend experienced when her brother was gunned down. During the days of grieving that followed, my friend realized the things that had become so important to her were worth nothing in her time of anguish. They had no lasting or healing qualities. Only Jesus could help. When she realized this, her "first love" awakened.

Another friend of mine told me she found spiritual renewal during another kind of crisis. One of her children left the church and Christ. This mother, in her heartbreak, turned to God for comfort and help. She started to read God's Word regularly again and to pray each day. As a result, she saw her spiritual life deepen and her love for others grow. Today she helps other Christians who face a similar loss.

Esther Sanger is another woman I know who faced still another kind of crisis that deepened her spiritual life. We call it the mid-life crisis.

She had come to know Christ as her Savior as a young person and had felt God's call to missions in her early 20s. However, she rationalized she wasn't ready, so the call got "shelved." In the years that followed, she became a nurse, worked as a journalist, got married, and raised a family. She also faithfully attended church. On Sunday morning, Sunday evening, and prayer meeting night, she found her usual place. And she was available to work wherever her church needed her. She says, "I was a good, saved, and sanctified Nazarene."

No one would have thought anything was wrong with her spiritual life. No one but her. She came to realize something was very wrong.

She started doubting the existence of her own spiritual identity. She wondered if she was a religious android who had simply been programmed by the expectations, beliefs, and life-styles of those she lived and worshiped with.

She says, "As I grew to maturity, I needed my own spiritual identity."

The next two years were difficult as she reevaluated who she was, what she believed, and what God wanted her to do with the rest of her life. She says the self-probing was a frightening experience because she discovered emotions and attitudes of which she had not been aware. But as she turned those feelings over to the Lord, she came to a renewed relationship with Him, a relationship she knew was her very own.

With this relationship came the desire to find out what God, not anyone else, wanted her to do with her life.

As she prayed, she was overcome with a strange, almost mystical impression. She sensed God telling her to do something very much out of character for her, something that some of her friends would think was bizarre. She felt God directing her to put a sign on a telephone pole. The sign she posted simply read, "If you need to talk to someone, call this telephone number."

People who needed help started to call. Because of her involvement with the needs of people, she realized the city needed a crisis center. So she started one, with $26.00 of her own money. It is the Quincy Crisis Center, of which she is the executive director. It now has a yearly budget of about $1 million.

Some people call Esther the Mother Teresa of the South Shore (the area of Massachusetts south of Boston). She is someone needy people can turn to for compassion and help—the homeless, abused women and children, the frightened AIDS victims, the elderly, anyone desperate for help.

All of this unique ministry came to life because a Christian woman wanted a personal, spiritual revival.

Career changes often spark a period of soul-searching and, for some, real spiritual renewal. It did for Margy Meredith, a retiring lieutenant colonel and nurse in the air force. During her years in carrying ever-increasing responsibilities, this graduate of a Christian college had lost her relationship with Christ. Now, when she needed direction, she had none.

She called her longtime college friend, Blanche Gressett, and shared her feelings of anxiety and apprehension.

Blanche lived in another town and prayed about how

to help her friend. She and her husband decided to stop and see Margy on their way to a denominational meeting in another state. Blanche and Margy had a long talk as Blanche shared her faith in the Christ who could help. When leaving, Blanche felt impressed to give her friend *Something More,* by Catherine Marshall. This was a book that had helped her and one she hoped would help her friend.

A few days later Margy called to give Blanche the news that Jesus was once again first in her life.

The direction Margy got for her life was that she was simply to serve wherever people needed her. So she asked the Lord to show her where this was. And He did. Since Margy's retirement she has used her nursing skills to take care of sick friends as well as serve as camp nurse at summer camps and retreats at the district campground.

She has considered no task that needed done as beneath her. When helping in the kitchen at the campground, she said, laughingly, "If my friends in the air force could only see me now—eight hours of K.P. duty."

Recently she and her friend, Blanche, started and now run the camp bookstore. The Book Nook is open year-round for every camp and retreat held there. Working long hours and taking no pay, these two women are making an important contribution to the camp, both financially and spiritually.

Spiritual renewal can also come to committed Christians who wouldn't say they have lost their "first love" but who are just not experiencing much joy.

For these people, Paul suggests a possible solution in Philemon 6. "I pray that you may be active in sharing your faith, so that you will have a full understanding of every good thing we have in Christ."

My husband and I found this true. About 20 years ago we attended a retreat for personal evangelism training.

There we decided to go out on visitation at least one night a week and to pray for opportunities to tell others about Jesus.

My husband was the Sunday School superintendent in our church, so we chose to visit parents of children who attended Sunday School. One family had two young boys, but the parents had rarely come to church—and so, a bit apprehensively, we knocked on their door. The boys were delighted we had come to see them. And after a few visits the parents came to think of us as friends.

As we continued our visits there, we prayed for an opportunity to talk with the parents about Christ. Finally one evening it came. The boys were in bed, the wife was out for the evening, and unknown to us the father was scheduled for surgery two days later. During our visit, my husband was able to turn the conversation to spiritual topics. That night we saw the father of our two Sunday School boys accept Jesus as his Savior.

The whole family started to attend church together, and in a few weeks the mother turned her life over to Christ at the close of a morning service. As this family grew spiritually, their joy became ours also. When we share our faith, we reexperience, through others, the good news of salvation available through Christ. And our spirits are renewed.

Renewal or Rest?

One caution. Sometimes when we think we need renewal, all we really need is rest. Extended physical exertion and emotional stress can drain anyone of all feeling—including the sense of God's presence. So the problem may not be a spiritual one.

If we believe our desire and commitment to follow Christ hasn't lessened, we may need to look for physical and emotional renewal rather than spiritual renewal. A vacation away from stress and responsibilities could help. But since this is not always feasible, we may need to get a bit more creative.

The wife of a Christian counselor told me that when they don't have time for a vacation, they take what they call minivacations. For this couple the minivacation is often just a few hours from a busy schedule to go to a nearby park with a picnic lunch. Minivacations can be a hike in the woods, a walk along the seashore, a bike ride, going to a ball game, reading a book. They can be anything that relaxes us.

3 Steps to Renewal

Remember the words, "I am the resurrection and the life. He who believes in me will live, even though he dies" (John 11:25)? We usually associate this with life after death. But that same Resurrection power is what can bring new vitality to the Christian who feels religion has become dull and routine.

There is hope for those who cry out with the Psalmist, "Restore to me the joy of your salvation" (51:12). If we feel we are at a low point in our spiritual lives, there are three steps we can take.

First, we should look to Jesus. Hebrews 12:3 says, "Consider him who endured such opposition from sinful men, so that you will not grow weary and lose heart." Jesus, too, faced the problems of life. And it is He who is the "author and perfecter of our faith" (v. 2).

Second, recall the spiritual height from which we have fallen, and repent. That was Christ's advice to the Ephesian church in Revelation 2:5: "Remember the height from which you have fallen! Repent and do the things you did at first."

Third, share your faith with others. We become stagnant when we fail to take seriously the words of Jesus in

Mark 16:15. "Go into all the world and preach the good news to all creation." Renewing joy comes when we share Christ with others.

As we turn to God when our spiritual vigor seems low, we have the promise He gave to His people long ago, "I will refresh the weary and satisfy the faint" (Jeremiah 31:25).

The One who loves us beyond measure wants to give us the refreshment we need.

Ann Cubie Rearick is associate pastor of Community Church of the Nazarene, Massapequa Park, N.Y., and director of pastoral care for Hospice Care of Long Island.

Chapter 13

Trust:
Letting God Be God

by Ruth Wood Vaughn

Background Scripture: Proverbs 3:5-6; Isaiah 43:18-19;
John 14:1-3

I WAS TERRIFIED.
It was noon on an ordinary day.
I was 15 years old.
I had danced in from high school to declare the wonders

of the upcoming debate tournament where I was certain I would win superior ratings for my articulate, mature logic.

My parents smiled quietly as they listened to the whooshing Niagara of their exuberant, youthful word-person.

And then it happened.

With no warning, my mother slumped in unconsciousness. My father grabbed her and told me to call the doctor. He came, carefully worked with my mother, studied her responses, then somberly said: "This is serious."

My mind fogged.

Could it be that, in this moment on an ordinary day, our lives were changing forever? Could it be that, when this moment became clear, life, as we knew it, would never, ever, be the same?

Stunned, I watched my beloved, beautiful mother as she lay helpless, unsmiling, unknowing.

Bewildered, I listened to the austere doctor speak an alien vocabulary. He was not certain what caused my mother's collapse. But as I recall the event, it seems like it may have been a stroke. All the doctor knew for sure was that whatever had happened, it had damaged Mother's ability to move about freely.

I looked at the expression on the face of my Gibraltar Rock-father and understood how serious this was.

In that moment I knew my secure, carefree past was rushing out of that small Nazarene parsonage without even a reflective moment for a wave good-bye.

I stood in that instant as swollen streams of lost past and unknown future rose, surged, and flooded the present. There was no time for preparation, no time to gain solid footing, no time to scream: "No! Time, stop! No! No! Let me keep the precious past. Don't make my security shiver into bits as I confront an unexpected, unknown, unwanted change. Future, stop! Don't rush to me! *I DON'T WANT YOU NOW!*"

When the doctor left, we stood, adult, wise father and youthful, ignorant daughter. We looked at the still silent form of the woman whose beauty had illuminated our lives. Swaggering in to stand beside us was the knowledge that my father's small salary offered no money for hospitalization.

I hurtled into shrieking, hysterical tears.

My father took me in his great arms, held me against the warm and steady beat of his heart, put his hand on my curls, and said: "Shhhh! Shhhh! Steady, Ruth, steady."

And then he said a phrase I had heard many times before: "Let God be God. We are safe there."

I pulled back from him, then replied in all the fierce ardor of teenage fury: *"SAFE!* Don't talk to me about safety. I know about our finances. I know why my mother is not in a hospital. Daddy, I know she may die. And you tell me to *LET GOD BE GOD! DADDY!*"

His eyes rested gently upon me. It seemed they understood all the pain of the world. Yet in the mystery of human anguish, my father dared to believe God, to obey God, to walk into a future he could not see, to step onto a road he could not know. He dared to face reality that made *NO* sense, yet trusting the God who, sometimes, allows us to be cut off from our past, cut off from our future, and stand on a no-man's-land of earthquaking limbo.

How could my father be so trusting? By the standards of many, he was a simple man. He was born in poverty on a Texas farm. Concluding his education in a one-room school, he had felt God's call to the ministry. He had given up farm, kindred, and security to make his life as a pastor in a new denomination called the Church of the Nazarene. He worked in tiny parishes where his pay was small, sometimes nonexistent.

Now his wife lay in a bed, where she remained unconscious for a couple of hours. I walked away from my father and moved over to the bed. Mother's face on the white pillow had a quiet radiance; there was something undefeatable in the tilt of her chin; the sweet, full mouth, the proud sweep of her hair back from the forehead.

She had given me birth at the age of 44. Now, at the age of 59, maturity and life sorrows had only accentuated the beauty, the courage, the sweetness, highlighting them with wrinkles and shadows.

Daddy moved to stand with me, his arms about my shoulders. "Little girl, let God be God," softly spoke the masculine voice. I held very still in his arms and was at rest.

Faith in God, like my parents had, was not something one can smell or taste or weigh in the hands, or buy, or pick off a tree. But it is something rapturous and real.

My parents, trusting God as God, lived in relative poverty, but were stronger, more unconquerable than royalty. I had lived in that regal majesty all of my life.

And now their faith held me steady.

Cut off from the known past, cut off from the unknown future, yet I knew I was safe.

God was God.

I would allow Him to be Creator, I the created.

I would allow Him to be Infinite, I the finite.

I would allow Him to be Father, I the child.

After Mother collapsed, she needed a wheelchair or walker for the rest of her life. Three years after this, she was diagnosed as having Parkinson's disease. She lived for about 14 years with its liabilities and problems: her hands were always shaking, and she would often fall.

But she kept her humor and her trust in God. I remember one day when I tried to roll her over in her bed. She rolled right off the bed and face first onto the concrete floor. I ran to the nearby hospital and got two orderlies to help me pick her up. After we did, the first thing she said was, "And great was the fall thereof."

I remember also asking her why she wasn't angry about her physical condition. She had a lot to be angry about. For example, on the advice of a dentist, she had all her teeth pulled because he thought they might be poisoning her system. But her teeth were all in perfect condition. After that, I had to grind up her food for her.

Mother said the reason she wasn't angry was because, "My life is so cushioned with gratitude." She focused her attention on her husband's and children's love and that they were serving God.

At age 76, after a 13-month coma, she went to heaven. My father looked at us children and whispered past soft tears: "She's happy."

My military colonel brother, Joe, leaped up at the words and said: "Yes, she is. If what you have preached all our lives is true, Daddy, Mother is running for the first time in years, singing for the first time in months, greeting Jesus and her loved ones."

And we who loved her gathered close together, rejoicing in her release, holding hands tightly for strength in our stark, earthly loss.

Calendar pages flipped. I learned more of unexpected moments. In 1974 I was diagnosed as having pituitary failure. I dropped down to 80 pounds. I suffered from stomach pains, rashes, and overwhelming weariness. I felt like water ran in my veins. I would work at my typewriter, then lie on the floor for a second wind. If it didn't come, I went to bed.

I had been a whirling, dynamic, achieving university professor, published author, wife, mother. And now, for myself, I faced my mother's moment. There was no possibility of shouting: "Time, stop! No, past, don't go! No, future, don't come! Known security, oh, don't change!"

It was no-man's-land again: cut off from my past, cut off from my future.

Later, I recovered enough to write two books detailing the spiritual journey with God in that earthquaking season when, once again, I stood in bewildered helplessness. Like my parents, I chose to let God be God. I chose to trust, to obey, to follow in the dark, in the silence, in the mystery of no human logic for this destruction of my past and my future.

Then, in 1983, my world blew up with a force that made slivers of every life element I had known and planned for.

My husband, an associate pastor in a Nazarene church, told me our marriage was over and he was leaving the ministry. My marriage died, and my financial security dissolved.

Within days after that I had a new pituitary crisis that chained me to my bed—a stroke that produced aphasia. This disease strips its victim of communication skills. I could talk, but my words didn't make sense. I could hear others, but their words didn't make sense. I could type, but my writing was incoherent. I had spent my life communicating in the vibrant people-world I loved so dearly. Now I was barred from it.

Brokenness . . . Brokenness . . . Everywhere.

I lay in my bed and surveyed a lifetime of debris. And was at peace. Yes, I was. No fairy tale this. No pie in the sky this.

I faced the reality of unexpected desertion and disability. And I, as Ruth, held steady, secure, safe.

Why? How could such impossibility of heart response be possible?

The memory of a man of God who, in my 16th year, said: "Let God be God. We are safe there."

I believed it as a teenager.

I now believed it in maturity.

My exterior world, in every known and trusted element, had collapsed. Yet I sat on the solid foundation of faith and dared to trust . . . even there . . . even though.

Early I was taught to understand that it matters not what another may do to me or leave undone.

It matters not the exterior circumstances of my world.

It matters not the injustice, the absurdity, the total lack of human logic of life events.

When I allow God to be God, I am safe. I believe it because I have seen it in the lives of my parents. And I have lived it myself.

I sit at my computer now and ponder the words recorded in Isaiah 43:18-19:

"Forget the former things; do not dwell on the past. See, I am doing a new thing!"

I have let God be God these past several years of earth-quaking loss, when the future was as elusive as a moonbeam.

I have trusted, obeyed in the shower of lifetime debris, dimly beginning to perceive that sometimes God allows destruction so that He may fulfill.

My life is an object lesson to a hurting, reeling, disillusioned world that when one chooses—deliberately, determinedly chooses—to let God be God, one is always safe. And in the fullness of time, out of the ashes of the old, the Almighty is "doing a new thing! Now it springs up; do you not perceive it? I am making a way in the desert and streams in the wasteland."

After marital brokenness, the dream lives on. My two children serve God with radiant testimonies. One is a Nazarene minister. The other works with in-flight magazines for five airlines, using his inherited "gift of words."

After physical depletion, there is now strength to traverse the nation as a lamp to others who enter the shadowy gulf of human pain, loss, despair.

After aphasia destruction, there are words again reeling out the manuscript of my 40th book.

That says it, doesn't it?

I dare to believe God would not waste a single taste of the bitter cup that has been mine.

As a tiny child, I learned to lisp: "Trust in the Lord with all thine heart; and lean not unto thine own understanding. In all thy ways acknowledge him, and he shall direct thy paths" (Proverbs 3:5-6, KJV).

As a 55-year-old veteran of life, I want to tell you the words are true.

As I let God be God, I am safe. I am secure.

Ruth Vaughn is a communication specialist who has taught classes in drama and creative writing at Southern Nazarene University and is writing her 40th book. She lives and writes in Bethany, Okla.